4-

SELF
AWARENESS
THROUGH
HUNA

SELF AWARENESS THROUGH HUNA

By
DR. ERIKA S. NAU

A UNILAW LIBRARY BOOK
Donning
Virginia Beach/Norfolk

Note: All names of persons mentioned, except reference authorities, are fictitious to retain the anonymity for the good of all concerned.

Copyright © 1981 by Erika S. Nau

Library of Congress Cataloging in Publication Data:

Nau, Erika S.
  Self-awareness through huna—Hawaii's ancient wisdom.

  (A Unilaw library book)
  Includes bibliographical references and index.
  1. Occult sciences. 2. Occult sciences—Hawaii.
I. Title. II. Title: Huna—Hawaii's ancient wisdom.
BF1999.N35   131   80-27842
ISBN O-89865-099-2

Printed in the U.S.A.

dedicated to Helen, who introduced me to the Huna way of Life

Table of Contents

Foreword

Back in 1968, Max Freedom Long told me that the Huna philosophy contained true secrets of real magic. He said that the secrets were workable, practical, and extremely usable. Then he asked me if I would consider the task of presenting certain of the essences of his life-long study of the mysteries of the Kahuna, the magician-priests of Hawaii, into a single book to be aimed at the mass audience.

My initial response was somewhat nebulous, so Max set about sending me package after package of books, tapes, and notes. We began a correspondence that became quite extensive. The eighty-year-old scholar was persuasive. "Huna offers the key to real magic," he told me. "It can be yours...it can be anyone's to use."

The more I studied the several pounds of materials that he had sent to me, the more I found that I was agreeing with him. The Huna philosophy was beautiful, and it did seem to offer a practical system of magic that might be utilized by any sincere spiritual seeker.

Secrets of Kahuna Magic was published in 1971, and Max telephoned me upon his completion of a reading and an analysis of the book to tell me how pleased and delighted he was with my presentation of his work. It seemed as though Max had been waiting to receive a copy of that book in his hands. It was as if that single volume would provide some kind of confirmation that a much larger reading audience would now become familiar with the teachings of Huna. It seemed that way, for a very short time after the book was published, Max Freedom Long said farewell to his years of scholarship and a lifestyle that bordered on the monastic and left the physical plane of existence.

In February of 1972, I was privileged to be the speaker at the banquet of the First Annual Aquarian Age Conference which was held in Honolulu at the Hilton

Hawaiian Village on Waikiki Beach. My topic, fittingly, was Kahuna Magic, the ancient psycho-religious system of the Islands. My talk drew upon the monumental work of Max Freedom Long, who devoted all the energy of his essential self to breaking the secret Huna code.

I pointed out that there were good, metaphysical reasons for Hawaii having been selected as the site of this meeting of Light Workers from all over the world. In esoteric literature, Hawaii is the remaining geographical area of a great culture that sank beneath the ocean, i.e., Lemuria, Mu, or an eastern expression of Atlantis. At the same time, the legends of several peoples maintain that a new and glorious age will be realized when East meets West in Hawaii. Surely, the state itself, with its ethnic blendings of several skin shadings and its interaction of many religious creeds, serves as a physical symbol of brotherhood and sisterhood.

Interestingly, the central thrust of my talk that night dealt with the principal theme of Dr. Erika S. Nau's present volume, *Self Awareness Through Huna*. I am delighted to see Dr. Nau applying herself to the realization of the energies and powers of Self which may be attained through a sincere and a serious study of Huna principles.

Then, as now, I am primarily interested in the mystical experiences of the individual. This has been true in such books of mine as *Revelation: The Divine Fire* and in the Star People books and research which I have been conducting with my wife, Francie. I fully agree with William James when we wrote: "The mother sea and fountainhead of all religions lie in the mystical experiences of the individual... All theologies and all ecclesiasticisms are secondary growths superimposed."

Many of those men and women who have responded to us as Star People have claimed revelatory experiences which involved a brilliant light that surrounded them. Such reports immediately bring to mind the account of Saul on the road to Damascus being brought to his knees by the blinding light from heaven, conversing with the voice of Jesus, then undergoing the conversion that transformed him from Saul the Christian persecutor to Paul the Christian proselytizer.

As we have learned in our research into mysticism, the phenomenon of the brilliant light heralding illumination also occurs to those revelators who have never heard the New Testament story of Paul, and it soon becomes apparent that the Christian tradition by no means has a monopoly on the experience.

Zen Buddhists strive for *satori*, the state of illumination which is attained by reaching a higher level of consciousness. *Satori* is described as the "godly light, the inner heaven, the key to all the treasures of the mind...the source of power and might"; and it brings the knowledge that in the spirit all are one.

The *samadhi* sought by the Yogi enables the Soul to become a lamp with a steady light which reveals that man is free, immortal, and one with the *Atman* or Universal Soul.

The Amerindian mystics on their vision quest seek the white light of illumination which reveals their guide, their secret name, and their mission in life.

So it was in 1931, shortly before he left the Islands, that Max Freedom Long encountered the light of illumination. He was, at that time, about to admit defeat in his efforts to break the Huna code. For over fourteen years the Kahunas had rebuffed him at every level. The Huna mystery was passed only from parent to child under vows of inviolable secrecy, and the few remaining Kahunas had learned by past unfortunate experience to shun all whites, whatever their avowed motives might be.

But then there came the night when Long awakened by having the mosquito netting which surrounded his bed flooded with a light so strong and so brilliant that it was quite unlike anything that he had ever experienced.

"There was no sound to go with it," he remembered later, "just the night silence. But I had a strange feeling that I was being subjected to some initiation or other. I just sat up in bed and stared and waited. In a matter of a few moments the light slowly faded and all was as before in the room...except that I was greatly impressed and set wondering."

It was after he returned to the mainland and was living in California in 1935 that Max was again awakened in the middle of the night by another manifestation of the Light and provided with another clue that would lead to his breaking the enigma of Huna. It was suddenly given to him that since the Kahunas must have had names for the elements in their lore, these words would be found in the dictionary of Hawaiian-English that had begun to be formulated in 1820. Since the Hawaiian language is made up of words constructed from short root words, a translation of the root usually gives the original meaning of a word. If he were to derive the roots of the words used by the Kahunas in the recorded chants and prayers that had been collected by Dr. William Tufts Brigham in his own forty-year-research, Long would be able to obtain a fresh translation which would disclose secrets that had been overlooked by disinterested missionaries.

What Max Freedom Long learned — and what Dr. Erika S. Nau carefully describes and illustrates here in *Self-Awareness Through Huna* — was the Kahuna idea of the conscious and the subconscious minds as a pair of spirits closely joined in a physical body which is controlled by the subconscious and used to cover and to hide them both. The conscious spirit (*Uhane*) is a weak, animal-like spirit that can speak. The subconscious spirit (*Unihipili*) does its work in secret, but it is disposed to refuse to obey when it holds a fixation that a certain action will bring about punishment.

Long's most important discovery was that of the *Aumakua*, the older, parental, androgynous spirit that has both the low self (*unihipili*) and the middle self (*uhane*) under its guidance and protection. The *Aumakua* occupies the level of consciousness immediately above our own conscious level and may be considered the "god" within each of us — an older, parental, utterly trustworthy spirit that incorporates both the male and the female essence. To the Kahuna, the Aumakua is the high self, the highest "god" with whom man can deal.

The Kahuna priest believes in a supreme creative force, but he does not believe that he can pray to it. The Kahuna maintains that humankind's only contact with the Source can be through connection with the high self.

The Kahunas had no temples or shrines. They had no dogmas that demanded the achievement of salvation. They did not believe that the higher beings could be injured by humankind. They did not believe that humankind could sin against a higher being. The Huna system held that God, the Source, was too high and too all-powerful for any human being to hurt by any mortal act. "I cannot sin against God: I am to small," the Kahunas would protest to the Christian missionaries. In Huna, the only recognized sin is to hurt a fellow human being.

At the same Aquarian Age Conference in Hawaii at which I was the banquet speaker telling of the ways of Huna, I met the great Hopi Medicine person White Bear, the same wise one who served as the principal reference in Frank Water's esteemed *Book of the Hopi.* White Bear recognized the ways of the Kahuna as being similar to his own spiritual ways, and he recognized the Hopi link with Hawaii:

"It is no accident that Hawaii is part of the United States today. It is a remnant of the great nation of my fathers that sank beneath the ocean. We knew years ago that our old land would one day be a part of our new land, the United States.

"Before the old land sank under the Pacific Ocean, our people were communicating with the great civilization of Egypt by mental telepathy. We accept what has been written. Those educated folk [archaeologists] who seek our treasures in the ground try to learn from them what we have and what we are in our hearts.

"Many people have said that our picture-craft is

nothing but doodling, but centuries and centuries ago the Hopi drew a jet airplane on a rock which depicted our people arriving from the birthplace of our fathers. Yes, centuries ago, we had a picture-craft of a flying saucer!"

White Bear went on to detail the Hopi knowledge of a coming time of cleansing and transition for humankind and the Earth Mother, matters which will be covered in my book for Unilaw-Donning *The Spiritual Teachings and Powers of the Amerindian Mystics.* Interestingly, Max Long used to tell me of the associations which he had traced between the Kahunas and the religion and culture of ancient Egypt. If we place this hypothesis together with a similar assertion by White Bear of the Hopis, may we begin to postulate a common seed culture for the Egyptian, the Polynesian, and the Amerindian?

"I have elected to call Huna a psycho-religious system for the reason that it includes so much that has always been considered a part of religion," Max Freedom Long said. "However, I consider Huna a science in the strictest sense of the word.

"The Kahunas knew nothing about gods. They admitted freely that it was probable that there were such Beings, but they were honest in saying that they were convinced that the human mind would never be able to do more than imagine them — invent them in terms of lower humans. The basic urge of other religions to appease gods or to gain favors from them (religion plus magic) is replaced in Huna by the purely magical operation of prayer to the high self for the purpose of gaining favors in the way of healing or bettering one's circumstances through a change in the predictable future."

I urge the reader to approach Dr. Nau's *Self Awareness Through Huna* in an attitude of openness and considered expectation. There will be those who may argue that Huna is a primitive system with little relevance for an age of moon landings and mass communications. But remember that primitive man is also basic man, and the eternal truths remain unaltered and ever contemporary.

In my opinion, so many of modern men's and women's neuroses have their origin in a conscious or an unconscious acknowledgment that they have muted their mystical communion with the unseen world and that they have grown apart from a sense of Oneness with the Source. It would, of course, be foolish to attempt to stop our contemporary reality of Space Age technology and to establish a separate reality to the exclusion of our fellow humans and our physical responsibilities; but we can learn how to deal directly with the unconscious mind and we can make firm contact with an order or a level of consciousness that understands existence as an organic whole.

To be primitive in our interaction with the external physical world of consensual reality would be to live in superstition and confusion; but to be primitive in our interaction with the inner-realm of the psyche is to live in wisdom and in spiritual balance.

May each reader remain steadfast in his or her spiritual quest and walk always in Peace, Light, and Love.

Brad Steiger
Scottsdale, Arizona

Preface

Huna is being widely recognized throughout the world as a fundamental philosophy, a meaningful psychological system, and a practical way of life. Those who hear of Huna for the first time either feel intuitively that it is important for them, or it makes no impression on them whatever. The most common reaction is that Huna puts everything they've studied previously into focus.

What Dr. Nau teaches is from her own experience. She is a certified Huna Teacher, a continuing student of Huna, and she uses Huna in her own life. Therefore, what she teaches—in personal associations, in classes, and in this book—is not mere theory, but practical techniques that work for her.

If you want to enjoy the full benefits of the Huna system, you must use it. Huna has been described as a "tool" designed to help us do the job of living more effectively. There are many theoretical ideas in the Huna philosophy, but it is the practical application of Huna in your own experience that will convince you that it actually works. Dr. Nau's book teaches you to use Huna. It is basic and the methods suggested are described clearly, so that you can benefit from them immediately.

Dr. Nau emphasizes two techniques from the Huna system that are particularly useful and are not readily available in other books. One is the effective use of dreams as a source of Guidance from the High Self. It is the study of one's dreams over a long period of time, interpreted with an understanding of the Three Selves of Huna, that makes this technique unique and exceptionally practical. She also teaches how to change your future by changing your dreams!

The other technique is the use of the characteristics and symbolism of animals to understand the low self. In Max Freedom Long's fifty-two years of research into the Huna lore, reported in his many books and bulletins, he

1

repeatedly referred to the low self as the "animal self." This is of course an analogy. Dr. Nau describes the technique of choosing the animal that most nearly describes the attributes of your low self. This method often transforms the low self at once from a theoretical "function of the mind" to a real being that is a vital part of you, and makes the team-work of the Three Selves more effective.

Self-Awareness Through Huna is a valuable addition to the literature of Huna, and it is an especially practical aid in helping you make Huna a Way of Life.

—Dr. E. Otha Wingo

Introduction

Seekers of spiritual enlightenment are told repeatedly by their advisors:

"Be ye renewed...by the renewing of your mind."

"Go within!"

"Meditate!"

The students' eagerness to cooperate is often countered by frustrating cries of:

"Yes, but *how?*"

"Where do I go?"

"What do I do with it once I get *there?"*

Many are frankly apprehensive, wondering about the shadows that lurk in the unknown. Caution is understandable and advisable, in lieu of historical retrospect.

Mankind has been searching for his spiritual identity since the dawn of time. The hieroglyphic carvings of the ancient Egyptians, cuneiform clay tablets excavated from the Fertile Crescent of Mesopotamia and recently recovered pottery paintings from the inundated civilization of the Minoan culture of Crete all acknowledge an interesting parallel: there is a vast difference in the priestly learning and the common knowledge taught the masses in most cultures of antiquity.

In later cultures, religion and magical cults and groups became fashionable. The aristocracy of the ancient world was dedicated to discovering the "true self" and becoming divine.

These teachings were rarely revealed to outsiders. They culminated in an overwhelming emotional experience in which the initiate identified himself with his god. He was "reborn" free of the animal lower self which had held him down. He had conquered death, and was assured a happy immortality. He had solved his identity crisis in finding his eternal identity. The climax was achieved through the magical, power-inducing effect of dramatic ritual as well as through religious devotion to the god.

The Gnostic sects of the Mediterranean believed a spark of the divine existed in man. It was held captive in the body and the evil world of matter. It could be freed from its bondage while still on earth to achieve its full divine potential. It could be gained through meditative visions in which the truth was revealed. In the system of Valentinus, the Alexandrian who taught at Rome in the second century A.D., the truth was revealed to the initiate by his guardian angel, who accompanied him all through life and who was really his *true* divine self.

The "divinity within man" surfaces in many religious philosophies, from Asian cultures to the Indians of the Americas.

The Essenes, members of the ancient Jewish sect of ascetics and mystics did not measure a man's spiritual potential by his material connections.

The simple yet profound philosophy taught by Joshua ben Joseph, known to later followers as Jesus of Nazareth was, in reality a very ancient "way of life" here called Huna. Some authorities are convinced Huna was the "secret mysteries" mentioned in the scriptures (but never identified) that Jesus taught his disciples in private.

Huna, meaning "secret," has surfaced under various labels in different cultures and civilizations of antiquity. Among the sophisticated orders it was considered strictly the property of the elite priesthood and taught only to initiates. In other cultures Huna was accepted and practiced by primitive natives, such as the Berber tribesmen of Northern Africa and the inhabitants of Oceana before the islands were "discovered" by western man. Where Huna was accepted as the native psycho-spiritual way of life, the people were the happiest, most carefree creatures on earth.

The Huna philosophy is simple, safe, workable and adapts itself with practical reason to our western culture. Made available to western thinkers through the teachings of the popular "mind awareness, development and control" courses, Huna studies have exploded with dramatic impact on all students of human behavior. The concept is simple to understand and easy to apply. Children take to it like ducklings to the water. Adults disenchanted by orthodox dictates see it as a refreshing alternative. It appeals to every age group and educational background.

Many psychologists who have studied Huna respect the Huna philosophy as a new approach to understanding human behavior for both the professional counselor and the layperson. Huna helps the student with his own identity as well as giving him an understanding of those with whom he comes in contact.

For, as thousands of enthusiastic adherents vouch: when applied according to the ancient principles in all sincerity, Huna works!

— Dr. Erika S. Nau, Ph.D.

Chapter I
The Secret
and How
It Works

The house was dark when I came home except for the dressing-room area of the bathroom. As I slipped out of my clothes, Tracy appeared in the doorway.

"How was the new development class?"

"Fantastic! It incorporates an exciting philosophy called Huna."

"Huna? Sounds like something served on a bun," she yawned. "What is it? Something new?"

"Huna is the psycho-religious belief of the ancient Polynesians, presumably dating back to Egypt, Babylon and possibly Atlantis."

I had her attention at last.

"Atlantis? Sounds like a heavy subject."

"It's simple, logical, and *it works!* Listen to this—"

"Can you make it in twenty-five words or less, Mom? It's one-thirty."

"The Polynesians believed there are two 'spirit selves' sharing the human vehicle." I explained from the depths of the face-towel. "A mind spirit, or 'middle self' and an animal (land or sea mammal) spirit or 'low self.'"

"Go on." The thoughtful look encouraged me.

"We had to identify our 'carnal nature' tonight, and I discovered mine at once. You'll never guess what my animal is!"

My daughter gave me an arched look without reminding me I had exceeded the word limit.

"That's easy; you're a dolphin."

I almost swallowed the toothbrush.

"How on earth did you figure that out?"

"Easily. What other animal pushes people ashore—whether they want to 'be saved' or not!"

"Look into the mirror and analyze your features," the instructor directed the following night. "Consider body structure as well."

We stole covered glances at each other. It was a normal assembly of students of every age, color and characteristic. Most of us wore a sheepish look.

"If you still can't identify your low self, make a list of your habits, likes and dislikes. EVERYONE has a low self. Society has chosen to ignore it till now. Freud calls it your subconscious mind," the teacher added.

"I feel like a fugitive from the zoo," leggy Virginia admitted with understandable frustration. She had a way of raising her head and looking down at the world I found fascinating from our first meeting. Her round eyes looked troubled. "Do you suppose I'm a cat? I'm not really fond of cats."

I watched her move slowly away, and suddenly it struck me. She had all the grace and gentleness of a giraffe—and she certainly was, as subsequent introspection proved.

Danny was a big man, muscular and strong, with a thick neck, a round face, and a bellow that could be heard across two counties.

"I'm a grizzly bear." he acknowledged, not certain whether this was in his favor or not. "Do you suppose bears like beer? Mine sure does!"

"I'm not happy with my rabbit," Agnes complained. "Can I change it? Why am I such an insignificant animal?"

"No animal is insignificant. Study your animal and learn to like it."

"I don't want anything to do with mine. It's a cat, and I always detested cats."

"You're saying you don't like yourself. Perhaps you'd better find out why."

Once we were aware of the animal characteristics in people, the physical resemblance soon became quite obvious. Some people literally "claw" their way through life. Others shiver and shake when spoken to in a harsh manner. You need only to observe those under the influence of alcohol or drugs to be shocked to startled recognition of carnal natures in action.

"I'm a buck deer," Tracy announced when she studied the Huna way of life. It explained in part her extreme shyness, and the tendency to run and hide from people and situations. Interestingly, she saw her animal first as a fawn, then observed him growing up until he sprouted a luxurious set of antlers. Further study convinced her the animal's positive attributes could be developed with patience and guidance, resulting in a more balanced and out-going personality—for the personality is our carnal self.

Not all students found their low self so easily.

"About the time I was convinced I was a horse, my low self turned into an impala," Don stated. "Now I'm convinced I'm an owl!"

He was reminded that the low self must be a mammal; one that gives live birth to its young. Further meditation was no help.

"Why do I get a whole zoo? Now I'm a monkey!"

"It's your low self playing games."

"What in heaven's name for?"

"It knows once you identify it, it'll be put under control. Keep up the search!"

We all tried to help him:

"Are you nocturnal or diurnal?"

"I can be anything so long as I have a nap."

"Do you like the water?"

"Love it."

"How about work? Hobbies?"

"I've worked since I was twelve. I don't need hobbies."

When he grinned his two front teeth flashed a beacon smile. Suddenly we all laughed, *knowing* this busy little fellow must be a beaver. But wisely we kept the thought to ourselves. The low self is more secure when the middle self makes its own identification.

Don came in the next night looking pleased as punch.

"I found my animal while I was shaving this morning." he announced airily. "There he was, grinning back at me! I'm calling him Bucky beaver."

Once our low self was identified, we were encouraged to study that self in order to train it properly. The reason was quite obvious. The training of an elephant differs from the method used to train a cat or a dog. Nor would a seal respond to the same method used to train a squirrel.

"Above all, *love* your low self." was repeated over and over. "Be firm in your discipline. Remember, this 'lesser' self is an intelligent spirit with a mind of its own."

The ancient Delphic precept *"Know Thyself"* (variously ascribed to Plato, Pythagoras and Socrates) was in reality introduced by a woman, the Greek poetess Phemonoe of the ante-Homeric period. Cervantes went a step further in his treatment of Don Quixote when he observed, "Make it thy business to know thyself, which is the most difficult lesson in the world." He might add it is often painful as well.

Some dolphin traits I considered flattering, others a little ambiguous. One brought howls of laughter from my family.

"The dolphin is an acoustical creature, capable of seeing with his ears much farther than with his eyes," Jacques Cousteau recorded in his excellent series on the ocean world.

My hearing is acute. Something within my head "rings" when a sonic-pitched dog-whistle is used by canine lovers in the park beyond our house. Significantly, my clairaudient faculty has been highly developed from early childhood.

Aware my low self is one of the most intelligent animals in the world, I have made no effort to put it on a leash or to coerce it in any way. We're "partners" and the respect is mutual. The Pavlovian system is used even so: when low self delivers something this middle self desires, it is rewarded generously. (And thanked!) Make no mistake about it! Low self lets you *know* what low self wants, and a word of caution is advised here. If you have a weight challenge, a hot fudge sundae is not the appropriate reward, no matter what your animal craves. . . .

Above all, there is love. Whatever and whoever your low self is, treat it with kindness, and be assured you will grow.

Summarized, the philosophy is simple and easy to understand, from a scientific as well as from a spiritual point of view. Huna teaches that all things on earth are created male and female, the positive and the negative, all striving to unite and come to a point of completion. We are reminded this is a world of growth and evolution, and wherever there is any form of level of consciousness, it expresses itself into life.

Huna teaches that man has a three-fold constitution: a low self, a middle self and a high self, frequently referred to as "the God within." The goal is the full union of the three selves, or triune being, to form a *complete* man or woman.

There are ten elements in the ancient psychological system. Translated into every day terms, these are:

1. The low self or the subconscious. It is a separate spirit.
2. Low *vital force* (or energy) used by the low self for operation.
3. The low shadowy body (etheric double) of the low self.
4. The middle self, the conscious mind.
5. Middle *vital force* (or energy) used by the middle self.

6. The middle shadowy body, inhabited by the middle self.
7. The high self, which is in reality two spirits, a male and female duality. This self is connected distantly with the low and the middle self. It acts as an "overself" or guardian and is referred to as "the utterly trustworthy parental spirit."
8. The high shadowy body of the high self in which they live.
9. The high *vital force* used by the high self.
10. The body: the physical body which is entered by the low and the middle self in their shadowy bodies, and used by them during life. The high self is distantly connected to the physical body, probably for the most part by shadowy "threads" issued by the low self from its shadowy body.

All selves have come up by an evolutionary process from lower levels. The middle self is always the same sex as the physical body and is the director, or one in charge of the lesser spirit. The low self may be either male or female, and acting as the servant self, does what it is told under the guidance of the middle self, who is responsible for it.

The high self, frequently referred to as "the God within" stands aside, coming only when called for aid and instruction.

The low self's form of mentation is very limited. The middle self has evolved to the place where its reasoning power is vastly superior. The more highly evolved mentation of the high self is still more advanced because it transcends both memory and reason, and is therefore beyond human comprehension in Its nature.

When they have sufficiently evolved in their progression, the low and middle self will both move up to the next level; then the low self becomes a middle self, the middle self moves up to the high self level, (joined by its polarity opposite from another triunity) and the high self moves onward into the company of the high selves beyond. A new low self graduates up from the animal world and takes its place in the new beingness created.

The low self manufactures all the *vital force* (energy) for the use of the three selves. Normally this energy is shared with the middle self, who utilizes it as "will." In "prayer making" the low self contacts the high self by means of the shadowy cord or connection, which it activates, and along which it sends a supply of *vital force* to be used by the high self in answering prayers.

Psychologists hypothesize with cautious excitement that the "carnal self" theory is a new approach to understanding the human behavior, only to learn the concept is a very old one.

The philosophy of Huna was once a vital part of the psycho-religious life of the ancient Polynesians, and it parallels what science has discovered about human nature only in recent years. The Hawaiians believed the only recognized sin was to hurt another human being, and free from guilt-ridden dogma, these natives were considered the happiest people in the world.

What is the history of the Pacific Islands?

Historians do not know the exact origin of the tall, bronzed settlers of the Hawaiian islands. About 750 A.D. they came from islands far to the west, traveling on convoys of huge double-sailing canoes bearing entire populations as well as animals, plants and the necessities to start a new life in a new land. There were subsequent waves of emigrants for the next five hundred years, and they brought their myths and legends with them, even as they created new ones.

The myths of ancient Hawaii suggest that the islands were once a part of a vast continent now submerged. The *Tumuripo*, (or, according to its alternate spelling, the *Kumulipo*) "The Chant of Creation" was said to have originated in the land of *Tu Rua*, or *Mu*. According to their legends, the *Mu* were the progenitors of the race of people now known as the Hawaiians.

The islands are the high plateaus or mountains of the submerged continent, it is alleged, as were other Pacific landmarks.

When western man "discovered" the Islands, he found a primitive culture worshipping a complexity of gods and "spirit guides." Man was a triunity, they told the missionaries, three spirits and one body. Actually, the Polynesians gave natural law personal identification with cosmic forces, as the "Chant of Creation" clearly demonstrates. Called "The Source" by the natives, their philosophy has been passed down orally for generations in a remarkably unadulterated form.

Some experts translate it to mean "the profound depths." Others said it was an esoteric term, sacred and secret, its meaning is known only to the Kahunas, the native priests, known as the "keepers of the secret profound depths." The secret lay in the understanding of man's mental and spiritual powers and how to use them.

The missionaries could not understand the three-selves concept of the natives and banned the ancient religion. Only in recent years when studies into the conscious, subconscious and superconscious mind were given the dignity of scientific research, has the Huna theory been given proper credence. But in the early days the missionaries decreed all ancient teachings were no more than superstitions and persecuted the Kahunas. They went underground, and gradually Christianity took over. Today there appears little evidence of the ancient culture—on the surface.

It remained for an American to bring the old philosophy out of obscurity and to tie in the Kahuna teachings with the scientific spade-work performed in the west by Jung and Freud.

A philosophy and language scholar, Max Freedom Long came to Hawaii to teach in 1917. He succumbed quickly to the native charms. Though intrigued by the Huna lore and the strange practices, he learned quickly enough that the secret sacred mysteries were "taboo" to the outsiders. He persisted, convinced the secret could be uncovered. After years of study, he managed to break the "code" when he discovered it was built upon the multiple meanings of root words in the Hawaiian language itself. Small wonder it came down the generations unadulterated!

During the next decade Long wrote numerous pamphlets. These and his lectures generated enough interest to encourage him to write *The Secret Science Behind Miracles*.[1] He wrote eleven other books on Huna, seven of which were published in his lifetime.

The work of Max Freedom Long is considered by many authorities to be one of the century's great archeological discoveries. Psychologists consider it a great contribution to humanity; philosophers declare it an invaluable study, suspecting Huna is not the simple primitive philosophy preserved by the native inhabitants, but a preservation of a way of life steeped in antiquity.

In his book *The Huna Code in Religions*.[2] Long boldly insists Huna may well be the "mystery teachings" referred to, not only in Christian scriptures but sacred works of other religions. These "inner teachings" from the past were known only to the priesthood and the adepts.

He admits the proper word for the "secret lore" has yet to be found; the code of secrecy was so strong, it may never have been given an official name. Possibly it may have been considered too sacred to mention, as the name of God in some cults.

The "secret prayers" used by the ancient Kahunas are also lost to posterity. But enough has been recorded by observers that a workable system of the ancient teachings could be re-constructed, and so it has been demonstrated.

Study groups were organized under Long's direction in southern California, and in many other areas of the world. Enthusiastic students declared unanimously that, when applied according to the recovered teachings, Huna has worked. Max stated only two regrets: that he had not the time to write a book of children's stories based on

Huna, and a workable textbook simple enough for a neophyte to follow on his or her own. In *How Everything Was Made: Huna Stories for Children* and *Secret Teachings of Jesus*, he accomplished both in the last two years of his life. He died in 1971, but his students continued to spread the Huna gospel. His books continued to excite researchers to further investigation, study and application.

My own enthusiasm went beyond the elementary class that introduced the subject to my small circle of friends and relatives. A search for other publications revealed little of promise with the scope of Long's genius, though considerable detail is given in *The Life and Teachings of the Masters of the Far East* by Baird T. Spalding[3] which was originally published in 1894.

There are some interesting allegations in James Churchward's books on Mu, particularly *The Lost Continent of Mu*,[4] but only from the point of view of the anthropologist.

The provocative *Gods and Spacemen in the Ancient West*[5] by W. Raymond Drake suggested a connection from Lemuria, Atlantis, ancient Egypt, and Babylon, as well as various American Indian cultures. There does appear to be a strange similarity of legends and myths, suggesting a common communications bond: Huna?

"The Huna Science"[6] is a series of instruction pamphlets following Long's general format. These encourage the student to use the pendulum, as did Long, for contacting the subconscious mind or the low self.

My opinion differs with the distinguished scholar only because in recent years the human mind, thanks to the commercial wizardly of Jose Silva and his mind development courses, has been likened to a computer able to manipulate and control the subconscious for the ultimate good of all concerned. In other words, the low self can be trained at the direction of the middle self simply by the direction of suggestology.

A small group was formed for united study, under my direction. As ever, when I research a subject, books just "happen" to fall into my hands. (That dolphin is a real retriever!)

"Hawaiian Huna" a series of tapes by Clark and Dei Wilkerson of California is advertised nationally, and may appeal to some students at certain levels of awareness.

Other reading matter referring to Huna teachings has appeared in fiction as well as nonfiction form. Of these, *The Penetrator*, a science fiction by Mark Harden, *The Wilderness Messiah* by Thomas R. Henry and *Wizard of Upper Amazon* by Bruce Flamb may interest the student of Huna.

One such was the delightful *Children of the Rainbow*[7] by Leinani Melville. It was a translation of the "Chant of Creation" mentioned earlier, including many beautiful old prayers and songs of the ancient Hawaiians. The book included as well seventy pages of "keys to the sacred symbols" with text explaining the drawings. Depicted were the Cross of the Eternal Creator, the *Tau Toru*, the triple cross of the Holy Trinity and many more. These have been imprinted on the popular Hawaiian prints sold round the world, few people suspecting their meaning or origin.

Enid Hoffman's *Huna: A Beginner's Guide*[8] offers nothing new, but the book is at least a publication on the subject of Huna. *The Miracle of Mana-Force: Secret of Wealth, Love and Power*[9] by Madeleine C. Morris is a simple step-by-step guide, giving examples and instructions for applying the Huna method to practical daily living. A long-time resident of Hawaii, Madeleine Morris made no reference to Max Freedom Long at all, the only surprise in an otherwise informative book.

Tracy put the thought into words one evening.

"If we must have a single practical textbook on Huna, Mom, maybe you'd better be thinking about writing it yourself."

It was the last thing on my mind, for I was involved in some complicated research on an historical novel on the American Indians. At last I agreed to "whip together" a series of lessons, sometimes finishing the nightly program minutes before the doorbell rang.

After six such classes, a workable pattern emerged, most of it in lecture form. This book became a reality only because many of the students wanted a permanent record to study and use as a guideline.

Interestingly, the presence of Max Freedom Long was strongly felt while the work was in progress. His enthusiasm for Huna reached from beyond the grave, which was not surprising. I could feel the presence of his pressure in my study, even when not working on the material.

Let me make it clear, *Self Awareness Through Huna* is not a book *channelled* by Max Freedom Long. My own designation is in the field of metaphysics, and all of my writing is out of the depth of my own mentality and experience channelled from Divine Creativity—as most authors will admit. Consequently, whenever the writing sounded too much like Max Freedom Long, it was torn up, and started anew. I insist on my own authorship; Max has had his turn.

For practical reasons, only English terminology is used in this text, though Hawaiian terms are employed (and explained) when and where necessary. My work with the class convinced me most students find it challenging enough to adjust to a new philosophy without burdening them with an unfamiliar language as well. Other authors of Huna may feel differently. Those wishing to use the original words, I would respectfully suggest, should remain with Max Freedom Long's interpretations. He is, after all, the original authority, and for leisurely reading, he retains much of the charm and enchantment of this beautiful island paradise and its interesting people.

The Picture-writing of the Kahunas.

Contrary to popular western thought, the Kahunas did preserve their ancient religion as well as the legends, chants and prayers in a unique form of picture writing.

These were sketched on cloths of *tapa*, a parchment-like material made from the inner bark of trees of the mulberry family by artists of the sacred priesthood.

These sacred tapestries depicted crosses centuries before the birth of Christ, every line, circle, triangle, square and dot of esoteric significance. It is from these sacred symbols of *Mu* that the Polynesian legends are preserved. The picture-writing of the Kahunas were their books of knowledge from which they taught their ancient wisdom, each a reminder of some bit of ancient lore.

They can still be seen today, though their esoteric significance is lost—in the brightly printed aloha shirts and dresses sold the world-over as "Hawaiian prints."

These symbols are a study in themselves. Observed here are only a few, as they relate to the three selves explained in these lessons.

Vital force, or Mana, so-called by the Kahunas, was often depicted as water because the *vital force* generated by the low self from foods and air consumed was just that: plain water.

Water raised to overflow (as from a fountain) was the symbol of the *vital force* being accumulated in a surcharge by the low self.

The *vital force* of the high self, originally taken from the low self by way of the connecting AKA (shadowy) cord, was symbolized by clouds and mist, which are made up of fine droplets of water. These, when falling in the form of fine rain, symbolized the return of the *vital force* which had been transformed to carry the blessings of the high self as it fell on the middle and low selves to help and to heal.

The tree and vine were also used as symbols, the roots being the low self, the trunk and branches the middle self, and the leaves the high self. The sap circulating through roots, branches and leaves represented the *vital force* or mana.

I found it most interesting that one of the symbols depicted, the Seven Serpents of Wisdom, was used by artists of primitive Hawaii when snakes are unknown in Hawaii prior to the coming of the white man.

Perhaps this signifies that the remote ancestors of the present Hawaiians brought with them knowledge of the creatures. The *Tumuripo* reveals in the fourth chant, that the now submerged continent of *Ta Rua* was infested with prehistoric reptiles of astounding types.

Max Freedom Long could have "found" the Huna code in their symbology. One such cross pictures clearly that man is composed of divine spirit, soul, and human spirit; that man has three different levels of consciousness which correspond with one of his three selves: the spiritual mind of enlightment is the mind of man's higher divine self; the soul consciousness, the mind of man's middle self, is the mind of the soul; the human mind is the mentality of man's lower physical self.

If, as Long regretfully admits in his last published works, "not all of the Huna lore has been recovered," perhaps some enterprising researcher will go back to the *Tapa* cloths and study them in all seriousness: the *answer* could be there.

This, then, is only a guideline to Huna. It is hoped that whether the reader is studying alone or with a group, it will help to bring him or her to a realization of his three selves, and a working knowledge of this sacred mystery.

Only through the recognition, understanding and acceptance of the mental, emotional and spiritual natures of man is the triunity put into focus.

Hopefully, *Self Awareness* will offer the reader the key to himself.

****

[1]Huna Research Publications, Vista, California
[2]Huna Research Publications, Vista, California
[3]Devorsse Co., Santa Monica, California
[4]Devorsse Co., Santa Monica, California
[5]New American Library, New York
[6]CSA Press, Georgia
[7]Quest, Theosophical Books, Wheaton, Illinois
[8]Para Research, Rockport, Massachusetts
[9]Parker Publications, New York

Chapter II
The
Low
Self

There is evidence in sacred and profane literature that the Huna philosophy was well known to the ancients. The societies who lived the teachings prospered and were at peace. Those who chose to disregard the laws were torn by war and internal strife. The principles were lost many times in the past, only to be re-discovered and lived again. The scientific approach surfaced in the mid-eighteen hundreds.

The subconscious mind was often the step-child of humanity. When the concept was again introduced by modern thinkers, the mental activity or concept of such an entity was challenged and denied. Today, however, most psychologists are convinced it is an invaluable discovery.

The Kahunas considered the low self a vital part of the triunity with definite functions. When all three selves worked in harmony, triune man was at peace with himself.

The low self is the seat of the emotions. It reflects love, hate and fear as well as the control of the various processes of the physical body excepting the involuntary muscles. The low self receives all sensory impressions through the organs of the five senses. It is the seat of memory. It records every impression, thought, and reflection. These are presented to the middle self for explanation and direction, for the low self has no sense of right or wrong. It also has complete control of the use of the low *vital force* or energy, and the full use of the shadowy substance of its shadowy body.

How To Recognize Your Low Self

Become acquainted with it. Analyze your features, study your body structure and your personality traits, comparing these with those mammals (land or sea, wild or domestic) known to man. If necessary, make a list of animal traits and compare yours with them. (Mammals are those animals that give live birth to its young.) It is not necessary to be fond of the animal you may be—and if you are not, be prepared to face yourself honestly! You *must* learn to accept your low self in order to achieve a balance of harmony between your selves.

How To Accept Low Self

Talk to it. Know that the two of you are in a partnership to work out your common destiny. You can only evolve together; one cannot grow without the other.

You must train your low self to work cooperatively with the middle self and the high self and understand its capabilities and limitations. If there is a conflict between the two of you, it is the middle self's duty to find out what it is and how to work it out.

How To Love Low Self

We can only love that which we understand. Understand *who* your low self is, accept it as a part of you, and know what it must do and why. Court it as you would anyone you are trying to impress. Remember, before you can love anyone else, you must first love yourself.

What is the Low Self?

It is a lesser spirit, referring to its level of evolvement, an independent, conscious entity, sharing the physical body with the middle self, which is also an independent, conscious entity.

Encased in its own etheric, shadowy body, the low

self is an exact duplicate, every cell, tissue, and fluid of the physical body and brain. At the time of death the low self in its etheric body leaves the physical body and brain, taking the memories with it. It takes with it also the complete control of any use of the low energy or *vital force* as well as the etheric substance of its shadowy body. This is the form psychics "see" after the physical body has been destroyed.

The low self records every thought and impression, storing these shadowy memories in that part of the etheric body which identifies itself with the brain. Sometimes the low self may hold unrationalized ideas which the middle self was not in condition to rationalize when formed. Guilt complexes may come up, and a sense of unworthiness bothers him.

An example would be: consider the child who has committed some small transgression, either stolen something from another, or committed a disobedient act in school. The act looms so overwhelmingly in his mind, he is fearful his parents will never forgive him, thus magnifying the act even more in his imagination.

The low self, carrying the memories, does not always bring these up to the middle self, who is not really aware of the situation. The low self may react so strongly to these fixations, the middle self cannot control it, and trouble may result. The guilt feelings must be removed in order to restore harmony, and sometimes an outside source is called in to help. (The Kahunas of Oceania were also the psychiatrists.)

So you see, the low self *is* an independent entity with its own mentation, independent of the middle self. Both have free will. But when they are at odds, we are truly "at war with ourselves" for the low self is literally out of control.

Note: The low self has three little known abilities which are totally lacking in the middle self, but are most important when making an effective prayer. These are part of its inheritance, just as are the basic instincts which include the ability to use the five senses. They are:

1. The ability to sense *radiation* from things, objects and substances when these radiations are of such a nature they are not registered by the usual organs of sense which give us sight, sound, small and temperature sensations.

2. The ability to form an invisible thread or shadowy (or ectoplasmic) substance of the etheric body of the low self. With this thread a contact may be made with objects, things or people by touching them, seeing them or hearing them. Once made, this contact is more or less permanent. After the thread has been established, the low self has the faculty of reaching out a projection (or finger) of its shadowy body substance, to follow the connecting thread to find and make full contact again with the persons, objects or things at the other end of the thread.

3. The established shadowy threads are used in two different ways:

a. The shadowy finger can carry with it a portion of the shadowy duplication of the organs of sense. When we die and live in the shadowy world, we see, hear, smell, etc., as we did in the physical world. In astral projection the *entire* shadowy body is projected to a distance, there using the senses and gathering the sensory impressions of what it experiences. These impressions are sent back through the connecting thread and presented to the low self through the use of the physical eyes and ears in the form of an impression or a mental picture.

b. The second use of this third latent ability is that of *reversing* the flow of impressions along the connecting shadowy thread which has been put to work. Impressions may also be *projected* (sent the other way). These impressions have been changed from the actual light, actual sound or actual smell of something, to memories of it—to *thought forms* of it. These minute impressions are stamped on microscopic bits of the shadowy substance, several of which may be joined together into a "cluster" to convey the several impressions needed to reveal what thought is about. This sending of thought-form clusters (instead of the actual sensations or the actual things sensed) is called *telepathy.*

It is most important to train the low self to use these three latent abilities in prayers because *all prayer is telepathic.* The high self of man is a spirit, apart from the physical body. The low self and the middle self live in the dense physical body with physical eyes and ears. The high self, to whom all prayer is first directed (by the middle self via the low self) has no physical ears. It hears no physical sounds. No matter how loudly and earnestly we speak to it in words, it has no way to hear us. Our one and only way to get prayers to it is through the telepathic sending of thought-form clusters of *the ideas embodying the things for which we pray.*

The low self extends a shadowy finger to follow the established shadowy thread to the high self. The low self makes prayer ideas of words in thought-forms and sends them along the activated shadowy thread. Unless the low self is trained to understand the use of this latent ability and to *use* it when the middle self commands, nothing will be accomplished. Therefore *to be assured our prayers reach the high self, use the tool of imagination: then practice it daily.*

The biggest challenge confronting the new student of Huna is "finding" low self. Ask yourself: "Where am I comfortable?" Are you attracted to "earthy" colors? Then look for your low self among the woodland or jungle creatures. Does the water fascinate you? This does not always indicate a sea mammal; some land mammals are as much at home in the water as on land.

What are your interests? Our seal is harem conscious; the chimpanzee (a computer scientist) has a delicious sense of humor. A dear friend who is a Siamese cat can literally "talk" to any dog or cat she visits, achieving an astonishing respect from these pets.

Once identified, do give your low self a name. I named my dolphin Lu, meaning love. Call it a method of programming, if you will. By giving him a personal name, a personal relationship is established.

By analyzing my likes and dislikes, personal habits and attitudes, I was convinced Lu is male. My brother once said, "Sis, you think like a man." Be that as it may. But I enjoy being a woman, and this attitude in no way interferes with the low self, nor does it take away from the middle self's beingness. In fact, I believe the difference creates a balance within me. Be assured, men, if your low self is female, you are of a more gentle nature and "understand" the opposite sex more deeply than male-males.

Physical characteristics also manifest in the body. Cats can be identified by the eyes and lines of the face as well as manner of locomotion. There is a difference between domestic and wild cats. Every male lion of my acquaintance would prefer to lie back and let someone else do the work—and how they roar for attention, even when they whisper! Female lions, on the other hand, work all the time, and every one I know manages a large home and family (efficiently) but also holds down an outside job and juggles volunteer work as well.

Members of the deer family are basically shy and tend to hide their light under a bushel. Males are more confident and aggressive, though training and evolvement have much to do with it. Cows move and think slowly; nothing moves them until they are ready. Seals are gregarious, with the female more docile than the male. Interestingly enough, the herd instinct prevails through the human animal in a surprising degree.

The Low self fox types usually reflect the vixen features as well as the characteristics of the animal. Rabbits reflect more the characteristics of the animal than the looks. Regarded as a sex symbol from antiquity, most rabbits have challenges in that area, though the more evolved ones reached out to the more spiritual aspect of the symbol, which is the Easter symbol of the resurrection.

Again, there are a variety of breeds within each animal class, though there are basic similarities. For example, there is a noticeable difference between Arabian horses and the quarter horses with the former more sensitive and high-strung, the latter sturdy, calm and adaptable.

Members of the goat and sheep families are also quite easy to identify, both in appearance and in mannerisms. The heads of bison, bull and ram are large, and tend to lower when angry; the goats are usually slender and agile and are bleatingly in evidence when annoyed.

Small mammals also reflect their inbred characteristics. Beavers are busy, squirrels are hoarders, dogs are faithful and loyal and may be fierce or docile, according again to the breed instinct and training. Cats are independent, loners and nocturnal. Bears must be studied for breed—for they vary from the cuddly koala to the fierce grizzly. Not all camels are grumpy. I know one with the disposition of a saint who teaches emotionally disturbed children.

One word of caution. Do *not* tell someone else what you believe his low self is. It is better for each individual to discover his own...and more fun.

Should the student discover he has an aversion for the animal he suspects he is, he must overcome his feelings and make every effort to court his low self. Without cooperation between the low self and the middle self, the person is literally a "house divided," and many personality challenges may be traced to this lack of communication between the two.

So do learn to love your low self. Reward it when it has performed faithfully and well. Pavlov used this method to obtain astounding results in the training of animals. It will work as well for you.

Chapter III
The
Middle
Self

The task of the middle self is primarily that of learning to work consciously and properly with both the low self and the High Self. Until we understand our three selves and know *how* they can be made to work harmoniously together, we cannot be completely integrated.

The Polynesians called the middle self *Uhane*, "the spirit that talks." This, the conscious mind self, shares the vehicle-body with the low self, and both reflect through it in the learning process of their evolvement.

The middle self is the seat of logic and reason. It works with the imagination. As a director, it must communicate with that lesser being to gain its confidence, love and trust. Always a positive teacher, the middle self must never indulge in negative behavior. *It must be in control at all times.*

This conscious mind self must be just that: conscious of the low self, which moves by instinct and reacts to anger, hate, fear and base emotions. The middle self must *feel* through the low self, with a feeling apart from the ordinary (or known) senses, the presence of God in all, through all things. This is a process of entering into God as He stands in the world around us, rather than one of entering into Him in some far-away heaven where He is pure Spirit. This is the seat of the intelligence, the intellect, the one which reaches for the finer things; the middle self understands about the high self, and is eager to give the high self its full third of our triune life.

The middle self must be patient with the lesser nature, treating it with firm and loving kindness as would a mother instructing a small unreasonable child. When the low self indulges in animal behavior and savagery because it is filled with complexes or guilt feelings, it may reject all help from the high self in a mistaken belief of its own unworthiness. Then the middle self must recognize the low self is out of control and offer it love tempered with logic in endless repetition to make it feel secure again. It is important to remember that both the middle self and the low self have *free will*, and may reject any help whatsoever.

Training the low self is simple but by no means easy to do. The middle self must instruct the low self by easy stages, using imagination, visualization, affirmations, memorization and controlled meditation.

When first subjected to meditation, the low self will be easily distracted; it will become restless, bored, conjure up a headache or even fall asleep to escape. Therefore short periods, repeated at frequent intervals, are better than too long a stretch of time. As in all training procedures, the proper tools are important. These are concentration, relaxation and proper breathing techniques.

How is your low self trained?

The middle self makes a mental image of what is desired. If the picture, projected to the low self as a symbol, is unclear or fuzzy, a low self will be confused. It brings either the wrong thing or nothing at all. When reprimanded by the middle self for failure, it will cease to function, in a frustrating effort to escape. *The low self acts only by instinct and at the command of the middle self.* Care must be taken *how* the command is given; always use the positive approach and gestures. If you shake your head while issuing a command, you are negating your desire.

If the picture projected is clearly and positively stated, and the symbols easily understood, the low self will take it to the high self and ask that it will be done accordingly. This chain of command must be thoroughly understood. *Only the low self can contact the high self* when such communication is desired.

Naturally this contact is impossible when the low self is in opposition to the middle self, so you see rapport is required. Just as the high self offers guidance and instruction if we will accept it, so that we may grow toward the next level of consciousness with its superior mentation, so must the middle self offer guidance to the low self spirit.

When we are in accord, or at-oneness with our three selves, our lives hum in harmony. We get our answers by "looking within" and going according to the higher teachings. A properly trained low self will bring us answers in dreams. It will call upon our high self for healing, for self or others. The low self is eager and willing to perform, if only we follow the rules.

Do watch your language. The low self acts by instinct, not reason. *Your every wish is his command!*

Saying "don't cry" to a child is wasted effort. He gets the picture of crying, and subsequently howls even louder.

Telling your dog to "stop barking!" is an exercise in futility. "Shut up!" gets results because the picture transmitted is an image he understands. Be aware both children and animals will pick up your thoughts and often act upon them.

Our dog, Duke, managed to get out every morning for a romp in the park, in blatant disregard for the city ordinance against such frivolity. Convinced all animals have a high psychic ability, I projected to him, and visualized his drinking bowl filled with water. I mentally suggested he come home for a nice, refreshing drink, reminding him how thirsty he was after chasing imaginary rabbits, and how good it would taste. Within fifteen minutes he was at the back door, giving me a reproachful look from the empty drinking bowl. He got the picture and came home.

Examine your everyday language for negative

expressions. Can you recognize your favorite among these?

"That just burns me up!"

"I can't see what he sees in her."

"I could just die!"

"I'm sick and tired of staying home."

Do watch your language. *Your low self is listening.*

The middle self must understand the animal self in his keeping. But be aware not all animals respond to the same training. It is the middle self's duty to study the behavior pattern of his lesser being and act accordingly.

Study as well the low selves about you. Be aware that a dislike for another may be a conflict of your low self with that other. The middle self must control the situation at all times.

Habits are important as well. Nocturnal animals have a different sleep cycle from diurnal animals. Land mammals differ from sea mammals in their relationship to land and water. Most wild cats are loners; domestic cats are home-centered. Thick-skinned animals are seldom bothered by cutting remarks. Deer and rabbits as well as many small animals are easily intimidated, reacting emotionally to even a casual remark. Understanding the low selves of others, then, is as important as understanding your own.

The middle self can *fear* only in a rational way. He can, will and should fear within reason (logic) the troubles that his death might bring to those dependent upon him, for example. He should look this fear in the face, consider all angles, and put his house in order, so that all is done to insure against such troubles, then go bravely ahead. Only when one has done his best to plan well to meet all possible emergencies of this nature can he have peace of mind.

It is true the middle self can be engulfed by the low self with a great wave of emotion and consequently overpowered. Waves of hate or desire, homesickness and longing may also engulf middle self. This is why *control* through training is so important.

31

Of all emotions, love is the most interesting to study. It is an emotion in which the middle self can most closely share. Basic physical attraction may be added to by elements of parental (or filial) love, and to these may be added the logical approval and admiration of the middle self, resulting in an emotional mixture of the most powerful driving forces on all levels of consciousness.

This is the purpose of the middle self: to instruct, direct and blend with the low self and to attain the state of consciousness wherein the three selves can and will function as a unit: "a whole-I" and, to put it so esoterically, become "holy."

Chapter IV
The
High
Self

The Kahunas taught that mankind was given endless joy and some sorrow; that life was beautiful and living was a *growing* experience. They called the high self the utterly trustworthy, *parental* self because it never interferes with the two lower selves, for this would rob them of their free will, which is their divine heritage and birthright. Composed of a male and female self, the high self is so perfectly matched and united, they are *one* — the Father/Mother God referred to in prayers of the ancients.

It is of utmost importance, therefore, to be cognizant of the high self and to learn how to cooperate with this spirit—like the middle self and the low self, it dwells in its shadowy body *outside* the physical body, connected with or by the shadowy cord or thread, much as a telephone wire. When the three selves are working normally and freely together, the low self, at the request of the middle self, can at any time call up the high self by way of the shadowy cord and give it a message. The low self and the middle self are privileged to learn by experience and must be allowed to try their hands at living without interference from the elder, wiser high self. The high self must be recognized and invited to be involved with our lives, for it is bound by law not to take from the low and the middle self the gift of free will. The high self will use the superior

.d power to guide us into paths that will make
, happy living, but we must *open the door* and invite
come into our lives and take its rightful place.

In normal living, the high self automatically gives the daily guidance from behind the scenes, often without our awareness. Things just "happen" right; difficulties are avoided and life flows smoothly, happily and successfully. Hunches and intuitive impressions come with a high degree of accuracy. Our divine Instructors come to us in dreams, offering guidance, healing and precognitive revelations, if only we accept these gifts and act upon them.

The ancient Kahunas taught that the high self of each man and woman is a god unit, and that through his (or her) own high self, the prayers offered were a call for the attention of the ultimate God-consciousness beyond our comprehension. This, the guardian angel, God within, personal savior, whatever we chose to call this higher consciousness, accepted all petitions on behalf of the lesser selves. The high self stands with, in, and above us as a representative of the universal God. There is no need to struggle for further enlightenment. All that is needed is that we recognize the high self as it is, and address our prayers to it. If necessary, the high self will attune to still higher beings if it is necessary to do so.

The three selves have a different form of mentation. The low self is the seat of memory. The middle self cannot remember, but can use reason to arrive at a proper understanding of what is going on about it. The symbology of the high self is *light* and *truth;* in esoteric writing the term is "the annointed one," and frequently the symbol "the way" or "the path" is also used. All these refer to the thread or cord running from the low self to the high self.

The high self has a form of mentation that includes the ability to remember, to use reasoning power far superior to that of the middle self, and to be able to see into the past as well as into that part of the future solidified or crystalized to a recognizable pattern. It can, with the

proper training (which is inherent in some pe
look into the past as well as the future of othe
then, explains the so-called psychic readings gi\
clairvoyants and seers.

The past is recorded as a permanent record. The
future is projected according to the thoughts built up by
the person's triunity, for each of us builds up our own
future, thought by thought, and from this thinking, the
high self builds up the pattern for our future. We attract
what we think about daily, be it positive or negative. If we
change our mind before the predicted future can come to
pass, we literally tear down this crystalized thought-form
pattern, and our high self must begin anew to build a new
future from our renewed thoughts. Such action is the "free
will" discussed earlier. We can all, at any time, change our
future by changing our thinking. Think of fear and doubt,
you reap fear and doubt. Think of joy and expectancy, and
joy and expectancy will be attracted to you. This is the
Law. The Kahunas understood it and practiced it daily.
You may do as well if you study and apply yourself.

How do you become *aware* of your high self, so you
may know it is working through you? Personal experiences
vary, but again there is a basic rule: Breathing—deep
breathing.

This rule is so vital, an entire chapter is devoted to it.
Suffice it to say here, this is a universal tool used in many
cultures and creeds to obtain altered states of consciousness. The American Indians referred to is as "the utmost
spiritual breath." Orientals consider breathing a vital
exercise in attaining spiritual contact with the higher
forces. To the Kahunas it activated the communications
system.

Creative Intelligence has placed conscience, a know-
ingness of what is right and what is not for man's highest
good within his creation. Within all mankind is the truth
about themselves and of their destiny toward and within
perfection. *But he must unfold it himself.*

Be still and know. To each will come his own

knowing. It may be a deep feeling of at-oneness with all; a peace and quiet. It may be a trembling or a flood of ecstacy. The eyes may fill with tears. The ears may ring. A surge of unexplainable *power*, rising from the ground through the soles of the feet and then through the body and out of the crown, may shake your very being. You may see the auric light of your fingers and hands. You may hear music, or smell a fragrance literally out of this world. You may feel a surge of energy or a flood of euphoria, a *high* that lifts you to dizzying heights.

This is the low self's contact with the high self, for the low self's contacts are through the five senses activating the emotions. When this experience is registered, the scripture *be still and know that I am god* makes sense—whether you can explain it or not.

Naturally because of the differences in ways of thinking, it is virtually impossible for the low self and the middle self to understand the high self fully. We can only try to understand what our limited minds permit, loving the godlike high self, serene in the knowledge it loves us at all times, no matter what we do. The high self stands ever by to respond to our call and to help us *when we ask for help.* We, the low self, are alone responsible for any limitations placed on the amount of help which can be given.

The high self has no limitations except as imposed by the low self and the middle self through failing to do their part. This is one of the greatest (and sacred) secrets of all time: there *is* a high self. It is standing with, in and above us as a god and as a representative of universal God.

All we need to do is to recognize the high self and to address our prayers to it. In its superior wisdom, it may be dependent to pass on any prayer request or prayer force to higher beings in the ascending scale of growth and evolution.

But! No matter how much we hurt or are in need, the high self cannot of itself reach out to help us until that help is invited. When we ask the high self to guide us and to take its rightful place in our lives, the superior wisdom power to bring us into paths that will make normal, happy living our reward will be lovingly and freely channeled through.

All prayer is sent telepathically to the high self from the low self, and should be understood. The ancient Huna test is applied by the reasoning middle self, to recall possible 'sinful' acts of the past. These must be cleared before a prayer can be answered. *If an act hurt someone, it is sinful. If it did not hurt someone, it is not a sin.* This test must be made by the middle self, and the conclusion accepted. If the low self has a guilt complex about something, the middle self must be aware of it and clear it up, even if outside help must be obtained.

When someone has a fixed sense of guilt, and is in doubt, it would be a good idea to do a daily good deed in an impersonal way without expecting reward or thanks. This is a physical stimulus that will subsequently establish in the low self the feeling that good has been done to balance the former wrong of hurting another. After all, the Father/Mother high self has evolved up from the middle and the low self experiences, and knows how to meet every problem that can confront us.

The high self, having learned completely its lessons of integration and union, is in a state of union with all the other high selves. These, the "great company of high selves" are an endless source of help and guidance and will offer whatever assistance is needed to put our "house in order" *when we learn to ask for such help* in our everyday experience.

Jesus, who taught his disciples the "mysteries " mentioned in the Bible, said that to contact the high self, you must get the low self to carry the message. Consider his admonition: "Whosoever shall not receive the kingdom of God as a little child, he shall not enter therein."

The Huna word of the secret language for kingdom is *Au Puni,* which means "the place of I, or the high self."

The root of *Au* appears in the name for the high self, *Au Makua*, or "I-Parents" or "I-Father." The reference "A little child shall lead them" symbolizes the low self.

Is it possible to "see" the high self?

Many people have seen, heard as well as touched the etheric beings representing their high self. But it is not necessary to do so in order to be attuned to them. You need only to have an awareness that "someone" is close. Accept what is right for you. If you truly desire to know your high self, such a request will be granted at the appropriate time. This is the Law. When you do so, you are not rising above the Law or receiving more than the Law gives to others. Rather, you are applying a greater use of the Law from your higher level of consciousness. This is what the Kahunas did.

For years I dreamed of a woman with long red hair. She appeared in over a hundred dreams (I have kept a dream record for more than ten years) in a variety of dress and experiences. Several mediums spoke of her and described her in detail. I was certain she was a relative who had made her transition before I knew her. Then it revealed to me in an altered state of consciousness she was in fact my female high self.

My male high self appeared to me one night about forty years ago at a group meeting. I doubted his existence, but many times he performed physical demonstrations that saved me from danger, once in a fall, another time in an automobile accident when I actually felt the wheel turn by unseen hands and guide the car across an ice-slick highway to safety. He fully materialized many times when I was alone and in the company of others. Unlike my female high self, who was only seen, he has been heard and touched as well.

The ancient Kahunas proved the high self had abilities western man could neither perform nor understand. According to their thinking, the high self can, either directly or through its associations with those of its level or higher, exercise control over weather conditions. They demonstrated as well an astonishing degree of control over plant, insect and animal life.

The ancient Hawaiians could "pray up" a storm when an invasion threatened their islands in the past. They could call the fish to the shores, as well as "talk away" the sharks from favorite swimming waters. Their "instant healing" process involved not only cancerous tissue but broken bones. Changing the future was a known ritual as mysterious as their dreaded "death prayer." There is also documented evidence of the raising of the dead.

When the combined effort of several Kahunas was involved, objects of great size and weight could be lifted effortlessly. It is believed by some authorities the Kahunas of Ancient Egypt were involved in the building of the Great Pyramid, cutting and transporting the great stones to make that structure possible. How this was done is not known today. Perhaps some day the ancient magic will be recovered. The apports of the seance room are a similar performance on a much smaller scale.

Science has much to re-learn.

The Company of High Selves

Max Long reiterated again and again in his publications as well as his private classes that not all of the Huna lore had been completely recovered. It was his fervent wish that a dedicated student would further his investigation of the ancient philosophy and share it with humanity.

It is my belief that those who have immersed themselves in the Huna philosophy and are living it according to its divine precepts, are doing much to promote their own evolvement. Many have passed their enthusiasm to family and friends. They have read every book on the subject and promote the Huna principles whenever possible. Thus, the "path" is ever widened and the channel becomes more pure. As questions are raised, information is shared with other enthusiasts, sometimes with provocative results.

Among my own students a question was raised with

persistent frequency. All those voicing this wonder were of a highly clairvoyant or clairaudient (or both) nature. All had been involved in metaphysical studies for many years. The question posed was: *"Does the high self ever change?"*

Let us return to our primary source of information. Long states in his writings: "God is unknowable to us, as were the beings beyond the high self to the Kahunas. The Kahunas believed that all high selves were so closely related that they could react as one unit, aggregate of consciousness, and thus take on the universal aspect, even while remaining individual. In Huna, we cannot pray *directly* to the beings higher than the high self. *We must ask the high self to exert his superior mind power in our behalf, and to send prayers of praise on to still higher beings."*

Because of my own personal experiences as far as memory serves me, I privately questioned this "recovered reasoning" on Long's part, but kept my doubts out of the classroom, till the challenging students aired their own reasoning:

"But I've *seen* (or *heard*) my high self! I *know* there are times a *different* high self comes forth!"

Questioning native Polynesians on this matter brought the usual enigmatic smiles. Then I remembered Leinani Melville.

In his beautiful *Children of the Rainbow* the young Hawaiian recalled the last conversation held with his grandmother: "Before the sun rises my spirit will be borne from its watery shell back into the kingdom of God. Tomorrow I *shall become your Autmatua....*"

How is this possible, you wonder?

The old Hawaiians believed that as a good parent watches over her children and grandchildren while living on earth, so does that parent continue the role from the spirit world after passing out of the flesh.

According to my Hawaiian sources, the Kahunas taught that it is possible for an *Aumatua* (an ancestral spirit such as a deceased parent or grandparent) to guard and inspire a beloved relative on earth.

"I shall watch over you from above and guide you righteously," Melville's grandmother promised him. "I do not know at the present time how this is done, but I shall find out from the *Hui O Aumatua* (guild of ancestral spirits) when I join them after I awaken from nature's trance-sleep of death."

The Kahunas also teach that the high self is assigned to the lesser selves at conception. Clearly the two selves are meant to work out their common destinies under the high self's guardianship. If a change of any kind is made within that triunity structure, that change must be made *among the high selves comprising the company of the high selves.*

Max Long gives this auspicious body only passing mention in the basic textbooks. Perhaps it is time my own revelation should be shared here with other Huna searchers. My own students are already cognizant of the details and most of them are accepting the information given.

Who are "They?"

The company of high selves numbers twelve, a significant figure in esoteric teachings. Each high self is proficient in an area of interest, profession and/or activity of the triunity's lesser selves. The contact is made through the parental high self via the vibrations of these lesser spirits. So much is accepted.

I have always been aware of "teachers" (identified by the intensity of their auric emanations) about me. It is obvious some have been with me for a long period of time, others are of more recent assignment. Of equal interest is the perception that at some other periods of my life other "teachers" appeared to be with me, and have, for reasons not explained, moved out of my vibratory influence. All teachers appeared to be involved in creative fields except during my brief military career. This is not strange at all, for my personal interests have been the creative arts from early childhood, mainly writing, painting and music. Interestingly enough, when it was decided I would add the full length book form to my writing expression, a few teachers left and others came through. Amusingly, when I was inspired to write several books with military and historical backgrounds, the high selves with such expertise made their appearance. Not the least of these "later additions" was Max Long himself—and what an overpowering presence he was!

If this informations smacks of spiritualists' "bands," so be it. They came with the light, and only when called upon. In fact, I humorously referred to these enlightened ones as my "Board of Directors."

When the Huna question of the company of high selves came up, I looked at that auspicious group in a new light. My logical mind reminded me that, since *this* was my world, created by my own thoughts, words and deeds, why should I not also have a "say" in the matter of my governing directors? Why should I not have the right to say *who* was in that company of high selves, since they were at my disposal?

Literally calling a "board meeting" by the calling the roll of my chosen "teachers" as my present life and work would indicate, I was nonetheless a little startled and pleasantly surprised to see *everyone so called appear on that inner screen of my mind.* So it has been for some time. The Law appears to work according to my requirements, and my life has never been so peaceful and productive. Armed with my new theory, I invited a former associate who was active in the film world to join my company. What for? My interest in selling some of my books for film prompts this sensible course of action. When help is needed, why not go directly to a professional in the field? Eventually, I know, my desire will be fulfilled according to the programming made—and it does no harm to have the proper push from someone 'on the inside.' Other teachers of Huna may not agree with me. It is their choice to accept or reject my theory.

As for me, the structure thus visualized suits my organized mind. I have moved comfortably within the framework of the aforementioned conjecture, and have reaped gratifying results in a communication as unique as it is practical.

To date only my own students have been made aware of this expansion of the Huna theory accepted by other teachers. Most of them are using it with satisfactory results. The reader may do likewise.

Chapter V
Basic
Triads

While it is possible to operate within the Huna concept knowing only the function of the three selves, understanding the process will give the student of the philosophy a broader base of operation.

In Huna, all things are triune. Three aspects are involved in the Huna philosophy and activated, whether in the field of healing or in prayer. It must be recognized that there is some intelligence wise enough to bring about the desired effect to change conditions when requested to do so. Some force or power to be used in making the change is in operation.

The three basic triads are mind, force and matter. There are nine elements in man according to the Huna philosophy, with the human physical body making a tenth. Mind is divided into a triad of three grades of consciousness. Force is divided into a triad of three voltages of force. Matter is divided into a triad of three densities of a certain kind of thin matter. The concept is simple and well ordered.

Since an effort of will or even hypnotic suggestion to the subconscious cannot be used, we must look for a higher consciousness, wiser and more powerful than we are. The answer is God.

Our minds cannot grasp the true nature of God. The ancient Kahunas said He was a triune being, and that between Him and man were several grades of conscious beings. The grade of beings just a step above man was so difficult to imagine and understand that efforts to comprehend still higher levels were beyond our imagination. These beings are able to use a form of thinking or mentation next in the line of superiority to ours.

The element of force: Since all things are triune, there is always (1) a conscious being using (2) a force or power, to work with (3) some form of matter, be it dense or etheric.

Vital force is the force used by the high self. The triune man has three voltages of this electro-vital force. *Vital force* has been, and may be measured in the laboratory. It is of the three to four million volt level. Similar force is found in the brain, but its voltage has been stepped up a million volts to the next higher level. The high self does not live in the body with the low and the middle self, and so has not had its voltage of *vital force* recognized by researchers. Huna recognized three levels, grades or voltages of *vital force*, a voltage for each of the three selves (or entities). The voltage used by the high self is higher than that used as "hypnotic will" by the middle self, so must fall in the five to six million or "atom smashing" range. Atom smashing voltages of electro-vital force, used by the high self, are considered to be the answer to how heat is controlled (as in fire walking) or how both heat and cold are regulated when the material substances in a bone-break are *dissolved to etheric form and then resolidified as an unbroken bone.*

Teleports in spiritualistic seances are produced by thinning out the substance of the object or dissolving them, then transporting it to some other place and re-solidifying the materials. Spirits of the dead are able to get the aid of their high self to produce apports and the phenomena of "transportation," levitation, materialization, etc. The spirits of the dead are no more able to sense and recognize and understand the high self than are we, the living. They have tried to explain the phenomena which they are instrumental in producing, but their guesses do not agree. In learning to use the Huna system, it is to be expected that the living will work with the higher self and produce such phenomena without the necessity of depending on the dead.

The vital force is made in quantity on the earth level. Plants have it. Animals and men generate it from the foods used, and air breathed. The low self in the body generates and uses the *low voltage of vital force.* This level of force is taken by the middle self, and its voltage is stepped up to the *middle voltage of vital force* which is used as the "will" to control the low self. The high self draws *vital force* from the body and steps its voltages up the *high voltage of vital force* to use in instant healing and other things.

The element of matter: There are two grades of matter or substance to be considered. First, there is the substance in a broken bone or a diseased or deformed portion of the body. This is the easily understood matter which is dissolved into invisible etheric form and re-solidified as normal or "healed" bodily portions.

The second grade of matter is that thin etheric substance of which bodies are made for ghosts. Everything has a thin, shadowy body which is a *mold of every microscopic part of it.* Each of the three selves has a shadowy body. Consciousness and *vital force* cannot work without material, so even the high self has to have a body, even if it be in etheric form.

During life, the low and middle selves interpenetrate the gross physical body with their shadowy bodies. At death the shadowy bodies are withdrawn, and live on in "the other side." The high self lives in its shadowy body all the time, never entering the physical body, but often touching it, especially during sleep. The halo above the heads of the saints pictured in old paintings represents the high self hovering over the saint in its shadowy body.

The substance of which the shadowy bodies are made is ideal for the storage of supplies *of vital force.* It is also a perfect conductor. The spirits of the dead can take *vital force* from the living and store it in their shadowy bodies. With it they produce psychic phenomena of limited kinds, such as moving tables, raps, and so forth.

The shadowy body of the low self is a mold of every tissue of the physical body. This mold can be withdrawn almost completely from the body for a time without the materials of the tissue beginning to disintegrate. This mold is not tightly filled. It has no fixed form, but can be stretched, elongated or made a different size. It is unbreakable. A bone may break, but not the shadowy body part that is the mold of that broken part. Cancerous tissues may invade the shadowy mold but not change it, So, *the process of instant healing is one in which the mold is emptied of broken or diseased tissues and is refilled with basic substances to conform to the uninjured mold.*

Chapter VI
Vital
Force Energy

The Kahunas taught that *vital force* power, *Mana power,* consisted of both positive and negative force. The positive works through the mental and spiritual; the negative through the material and physical. *All life is the union of positive and negative forces.* The highest represents those forces of nature that work for the benefit of mankind, and the harmony of nature. The lowest negative forces work for destruction.

Habits are built around positive and negative concepts of life. A memory that prevents a person from reaching his highest potential is not in the best interest of that individual. Such memories are called "outlaw memories" and are treated in a separate chapter.

Success and happiness are built from reality.

The positive force is the knowledge of the truth or God within man. Such are self control, patience, kindness, humbleness and love. The negative forces in man are his biological processes and emotions. Negative or material things of life are composed of emotional attachments which create negative emotions. These are greed, selfishness, lust, envy, hate, jealousy, etc.

To the Kahunas, all action takes place because of a spiritual being. Our emotions are the tools that spiritual beings of the lowest negative force use to control us. So

long as we hide from the emotions, so long as w
understand them, we are prey to the power of t'
negative spirits.

The highest of the negative power could be used by
the Kahunas to heal, bring peace of mind, and to achieve
material wealth. The Kahunas learned to distinguish
between the highest and the lowest of the negative of their
own natures. The Kahunas derived this power *by bringing
the negative forces into harmony with the positive forces.*

The Kahunas taught that the symbol of the middle
self is the forehead. The heart symbolizes the low self.

They believed the negative is centralized below the
navel and the positive is located in the center of the head
between the eyes. Between these two centers is a bridge of
energy that flows back and forth: one must balance the
positive and negative for health and true happiness. There
is then established a flow in which the positive refills the
negative and the negative allows the positive to find
material and psychic expression.

When there is a balance of positive and negative, *vital
force* power flows freely through the psychic centers of the
body and the haven of the spirit is flooded with light. Man
does not then merely reflect the light of God, he *radiates*
the light. The haven of the spirit is located between the
eyes at the bridge of the nose, but will fill the entire
forehead as man develops and obtains the inner light of
psychic sight.

You may have felt pressure in that area during
meditation. It is the "expansion" of the inner development. You literally *do* feel the light glowing within.

The ancient Hawaiians did not believe in sin.
According to their thinking, sin was a man-made law; that
is real only for the person who believe it is real. This
means, that the person possessed of negative emotions of
guilt, cannot be free. He is *sinful* because of his feelings of
guilt. His own mind enslaves him.

Vital force flows most freely when all guilt complexes
are removed, no matter what label we put on them. People

who have trouble falling asleep may use the relaxation method of meditation, and deepening their *vital force* power, actually put themselves into the sleep state by applying the heart rhythm breathing method described in the next chapter. Even if you do not "get a wink of sleep" all night, you do *rest* and recharge your system as you drift into and out of the different sleep levels.

A woman addicted to sleeping pills for five years following the death of her husband agreed to try this method, thinking she would have nothing to lose. Concentrating on her breathing, she vaguely heard the clock chime the hour; then sixty minutes later again.

"Next thing I knew it was morning!" she confessed in astonished delight. "In two hours I broke a sleeping pill habit I once thought was my fate for the rest of my life. It was painless—and inexpensive. I'm free!"

Sleep learning is not as improbable as it may sound. It is possible to tape affirmations or desired effects and conditions which may then be played back before going to sleep at night; sometimes even falling asleep in the process of listening to the middle self's recitation of our wishes. The *low self is listening!* The impressions imprinted upon the subconscious mind spirit carry over into the waking thoughts (and often nocturnal dreams) and eventually are collected by the high self as building material to shape up the future.

In sleep, the low self and the middle self put the body down to rest and go elsewhere. We all astral travel, but not everyone remembers these experiences. Conscious awareness of such experiences are a matter of training. Polynesian children with potential were taken in hand by Kahunas and taught "the old ways" and astral projection was one of the fundamental teachings. They were taught to gaze on a bright object or flower, and to repeat "I am leaving the body. I am going to — —." (naming a favorite place.) How soon they appeared outside the physical body ⸱and could observe it from a distance (or from above) would depend on their powers of concentration.

Suggestion is another technique. You step out of physical state of consciousness into another level of consciousness by using the breathing method. Focus on an object, a picture or on a blank screen. *Vital force* power will start to flow as soon as the breathing has quieted the physical body, for mental relaxation follows soon after. Be assured this is done under the guardianship of the high self, but *do* ask for that protection. Remember, no matter how much you hurt, or however much you need help, your high self is not permitted by Law to come forward unless invited.

How Does the Healing Work?

Whether for self or for others, be it distant or contact healing, the methodology is the same. The middle self must direct low self to request healing from the high self. The path must be cleared (shadowy cord) so that healing may be channeled to the one in need.

For self healing, and reenergizing, visualize the *vital force* power flowing to the psychic centers. There are seven. The first is at the base of the spine; the second in the spleen area; the third is the solar plexus; fourth the heart area; fifth the thyroid center; sixth the pineal (center of the forehead) and the seventh is the crown of the head. Direct the low self to bring a surcharge of *vital force* power to each center, sending it on a thoughtform picture. You will feel a glow of warmth, tingling sensation and a general feeling of well being.

When sending healing help to another, the middle self directs the low self to contact the high self with the request that *the high self of the one needing help join in sending the surcharge of vital force power* to the patient after the path has been cleared.

If the healing is by the distant method (absence of patient), simply visualize his psychic centers and send the healing on a thought-form picture with the surcharge of *vital force*. If the disability or disease is known, mentally project healing in a positive way by saying "Take the surcharge of *vital force* flowing into (the afflicted area) and cause it to become perfect and functioning in a normal condition."

When the healing is done by physical contact, touch the person's psychic center on his back by using the positive/negative hand-flow. Your right hand, if you are right-handed, is the "healing or sending" hand; the left is used as the alternate and placed on the crown center front, the so-called "computer" area of the head. Only for the sixth center (pineal) is the action reversed. This, the pineal, is relative to the "haven of the spirit" known to the Kahunas: between the eyes at the bridge of the nose. After the crown center is visualized and reenergized, go to the afficted area and concentrate the surcharge of *vital force* there.

Please be advised you need not think you have special healing powers. This method works in so many ways. Fathers and mothers may help their children, be it for a toothache or fever. Children respond most gratifyingly to contact healing, because of their faith.

Pets also respond to healing, be it contact or distant. They are at the level of consciousness where our own low self may reach them *without verbal command.*

Plants and trees respond to this healing as well. When my husband planned to dig up a "dead" lemon tree one weekend, I mentally projected healing to it several days before the digging was to take place. Convincing him the tree still had "some life left," I persuaded him to transplant it to another area instead. The tree has since rewarded us with a bounty of lemons with astonishing regularity.

Other personal experiences of distant healing (and contact healing) have afforded me some interesting observations, with consequent feedback:

The question is often asked: "Can you *feel* it when the *vital force* is directed to you as a healing energy?"

The answer is an unqualified *yes!*

The verification comes from a broad spectrum, with ailments ranging from mild bronchitis to a heart attack;

from major abdominal surgery to burn victim reports. *i* admit they could "feel" the energy flow. One described it as so intense, "I felt I was plugged into a vibrating machine."

As a spiritual healer attached to a church where the "laying on of hands" is a vital function of the service, I can assure you the healing channel *does* feel the energy coming through. Often on cold days, when my hands are admittedly cool, the patient on the healing stool is astonished to feel *heat* through several thicknesses of clothing.

Since the Huna secret behind prayer has long been lost, we can operate only by trial and error. Obviously, beside the "chants" memorized by the Kahunas (and passed down by word of mouth to the apprentice), breathing for the communication with the high self is a vital tool. The healer collects the surcharge of *vital force* and transforms it to the patient, inhaling deeply, then exhaling with lips slightly open to "direct" the breath to the one in need. Since the healer is using an extra supply of *vital force* power and *not his own energy* he should not feel depleted; rather he should experience a feeling of well being and an euphoric peace within.

Of even greater importance, however, is the removing of the guilt complexes or "sins" of the patient. These are often hidden even to the person wishing healing. Therefore, whatever healing is given is usually only temporary. For a permanent healing, the thinking must be changed, followed by corresponding action. Whenever possible, I talk to the patient to understand his problem.

Gloria came to me following a mastectomy. She talked freely of her "carefree life" on a beautiful yacht that was the consuming passion of her husband. An excellent sailor, she was his first mate and crew, and outwardly they appeared an ideal couple.

But it soon came out she was more than a mere deck hand. She had a rare creative gift, set aside for lack of time and the meditative privacy needed to develop herself.

Deep down, she harbored a resentment that gradually manifested itself into a physical punishment. Cancer is the effect: resentment the cause.

Recognizing the truth, she decided to watch her thoughts more carefully in the future, hoping as well to find some time to "do her own thing." She has not yet found the time to express her own creativity, but her strong middle self has put the reins on her low self. To date all subsequent tests have proved negative. Jesus put it succinctly: *"Be ye renewed . . .by the renewing of your mind."*

The Kahunas were trained psychics, or worked directly with those who were. Heightened to evolved awareness, their senses perceived often what the untrained (undeveloped) mind could not. Their claim that often *vital force* is "stolen" from a patient by a dispossessed spirit may leave the modern student incredulous. Psychiatry has taken a second look at possession, and many now regard their patients with new eyes. What causes disorientation? What is "clinical insanity?" *What is the cause behind it all?*

I would suggest the serious student of Huna be guided according to his own level of thinking, saying only: *do* read *The Secret Science At Work* by Max Freedom Long thoroughly, then proceed from there. As mentioned before, much of this is not so much a matter of *learning* as it is a matter of *relearning*.

This applies as well to prayers not answered. This, as was mentioned earlier, concerns the low self's inability to reach (or to face) the high self because of a mistaken feeling of sin or guilt.

As a child is afraid to face its parents when it has done something wrong, so does the low self reject contact with the high self, making the complete communication impossible.

Interestingly, one who hurts another maliciously but feels no guilt or shame, but rather triumph for having "put something over" on others will *not have his low self refuse to make the contact with his high self. Nor will his high self cut him off.* The prayer for help (request) will be answered because this is the Law. The punishment for such trangression? Also according to the Law. There will be a break in the evolution upward for such a one. *Justice is Mine sayeth the Lord (Law)*. The Law *will* be balanced; all in good time. We reap what we sow, sooner or later. In this mathematical universe, where polarity opposites attract, where all is cause and effect, where you cannot have one without the other, evolution is attained only by balance. This is the unalterable Law known to and practiced by the Kahunas. It is the Universal Law.

Chapter VII
The
Importance of
Breathing

The Kahunas have passed down to us in a vague form the information that the universe has been created by the *action of consciousness upon force to create matter.*

Mythology, which some say is nothing more than garbled race-memories, frequently tells us more of a race or culture than we are expected to understand on the esoteric level. In the Tumuripo, the Hawaiian Chant of Creation, a panoramic epic of spiritual poetry of unknown origin, the elements take on the magical properties of gods and goddesses, the philosophy disguised in esoteric rhetoric.

Science tells us that all matter is made up of an electrical form, force or energy which has been set into motion in certain relations to other units of moving force, and that, seemingly because of the balance between the positive and negative forces in any given combination, we have the various forms of matter.

Huna tells us that the thing which sets this electrical force into fixed motion is *consciousness*. The high self can use its consciousness to cause *vital force* to become high in voltage, and to cause changes in temperature and matter (as in fire walking and instant healing). Above the level of the high self are still higher levels of consciousness which are entirely beyond human conception, but which can create on a world scale. In other words, in Huna, we ask the high self to pray, asking it to pray in turn to these still higher beings, should such prayer be needed. In Christianity we pray to God through the mediation of Jesus, the Son.

It follows that, while the low self of man cannot use his *lesser* form of consciousness to cause his *vital force* to make changes in matter as does the high self, his control of the bodily *vital force* is still remarkable.

Breathing is the communication life-line between the three selves. Deeper and stronger breathing must be done to accumulate the *vital force* to be sent to the High Self. The method is relatively simple and easy to master

Take a deep breath to the count of four; exhale to the count of four in a series of four breaths. Wait about 20 seconds, then inhale again to the count of four, then exhale to the count of four. Continue this for ten series.

This is called the heart-beat rhythm, and you will find yourself automatically adjusting to it in a very short time. You find yourself breathing deeply and naturally as soon as you go into meditation, prayer or a healing action. By concentrating on the count, the middle self will automatically take the low self with it.

As you take the first breath, you command your low self to begin to collect the *vital force*, and with the end of the series, command this *vital force* be sent to the high self. As the *vital force* is sent, the prayer picture (or healing request) is visualized. Once this order has been given mentally, the picture of the *desired condition* must be visualized *as perfectly as possible*. With it may be given a prayer formulated and memorized (or affirmation) which should be repeated, three times slowly and carefully. The breathing will continue without effort. If you become overloaded with oxygen and begin to feel light-headed or have unusual sensations, pause between sets of four breaths.

Sometimes the flow of *vital force* from the high self

ı actually be felt. It is like fine rain falling on the crown or shoulders, or a tingling feeling in the palm of the hands.

Deep breathing is a common preliminary to telepathic practices of psychometrizing. Here the thought-forms are made and sent along the thread connecting the shadowy body to the object. Deep breathing helps the low self to relax and obey. Impressions come from below the solar plexus, long considered the main seat of the low self when sending or receiving messages of sensory impressions.

A different phase of telepathy is that in which distant settings appear before the inner eye. This is called clairvoyance, and occasionally includes glimpses of events that will transpire in the future. Again, breathing is the stimulus that activates the low self, and the high self that produces the results.

Deep breathing is most important in the matter of healing, be it of self or others. Again it is the *vital force* flowing to the subject that does the work. Even in the 'laying on of hands' breathing is the signal alerting the high self, and, if necessary, communication with beings beyond our ken.

The *vital force*, or bodily electricity, has an amazing characteristic which is still unknown to modern researchers. This characteristic is that it responds to the commands and direction of the *consciousness of Sentient Beings* almost as if it were Itself conscious.

It is important to note that an accumulating of an extra amount of *vital force* is very simple once it is known all that needs to be done is to *request* it. Simply urge the low self to breathe more *deeply*. *Vital force* is stored in the body, ready for instant use as required. This is what can be done during creative meditation. Those dedicated to serving their fellow man may thus store up a ready supply of *vital force* and tap it as needed, as did the ancient Kahunas. This is why some healers appear to have a greater healing channeling capacity than others. It explains also the creativity of some writers and artists using the meditative state, even when they do not understand the process and simply "go there."

Those who have studied the effects of *vital force* say it seems to be alive, appearing almost to have a form of intelligence of its own. This is not really so, of course, for *vital force* can act only when and as it charges and vitalizes shadowy substances. The consciousness is invariably that of the low self dictating the projection of what it is to do.

The Kahunas used the symbol of water for mana, or *vital force*. When they wished to accumulate a surcharge, they breathed deeply and *visualized* the *vital force* rising like water gushing from a fountain, seeing it rise higher and higher until it overflows. (The body is pictured as the fountain and the water as the *vital force*.)

An addition of *vital force* can always be felt, either in a sense of well being, of physical strength, will and determination or of an acute sharpening of the mind. This is also evidenced in visual perception.

Obviously *vital force* is the life force. Medical men have long known when the level of *vital force* falls too low, the middle self, lacking guidance, becomes erratic, then neurotic or psychotic symptoms appear. And if the level is far enough depleted, the victim may sink into a state of depression ending in insanity.

Therefore increasing the shadowy body substance by breathing, thus increasing the *vital force* charge, is certainly beneficial. When one has learned to accumulate a surcharge, it is possible to use it, and with the help of the high self, perform miracles ranging from slow and simple healing cures to miraculous changes in bodily tissues as well as changing the fabric for the future.

Practice this exercise daily. In so doing, you are keeping 'attuned to the Infinite' through your own high self.

Chapter VIII
Communication

The Kahunas called it the "aka cord" — that shadowy thread made by the low self as a communication line to the high self. Picture it as a telephone wire transmitting telepathy. It must be thoroughly understood and *used*, if answers to prayers (and all else requested) are to be obtained.

The shadowy body of the low self is not only a mold of all the tissues of the body, a storage place of memories, a conductor of *vital force*, it is also the means of connecting us with things and people. It is *sticky*. When we see something, it extends out with the sight, and sticks a tiny thread of invisible substance to the thing seen. We shake hands, and a thread connects us with the person touched. We establish a connection with it. Such connecting threads of shadowy body substance last for a great length of time, and tie us into our surroundings. They act as guides, when we order our low self to reach out and contact someone. Once contact is made, the thread is momentarily strengthened by pouring into it more shadowy body substance. This is projected from the shadowy body of the low self. The Kahunas speak of it figuratively as "sticking out a finger."

Coming into my room one night I observed an etheric figure in the dark standing at the foot of my bed. Being tired, I brushed the form aside, saying I did not wish to be disturbed, and suggested she leave. The form was of a substance as filmy as spiderwebs, and even as I turned away, I recognized my visitor as an astral guest, not a discarnate. When I mentioned it to her later, she admitted she had projected to me, but only in a general way as she did to all her students nightly. I must admit there was absolutely no difference between the substance generated by my teacher and the ectoplasmic substance produced by those who made their transition from this physical planet.

Once the thread is thus reinforced, it is a perfect conductor for *vital force,* and on a *flow of vital force,* or a current, thought-forms are carried to the high self. A portion of the sensory organisms can be removed from the physical organs and projected to the thing touched through the projecting "finger." Remember, the sensory organs are duplicated in the shadowy body of the low self. We retain these senses after death.

The shadowy threads bind the clusters of thought-forms together as we store them in series in our memories. "Associations" of memories are a matter of being able to pull strings attached to one memory and draw up all associated memories.

A thread, or cord of threads, connects us with objects and people often touched. Mediums sometimes can feel these threads from the region of the solar plexus. The mechanism of psychometry is to touch an object, then cause the low self to stick out a "finger" and follow the threads which are attached to the object, back to the owner. That person may be around the world in distance, even dead and living now in a shadowy body on "the other side"—but he can be touched. His thoughts and memories can be inspected, his appearance noted, and his surroundings sensed and seen. Practicing psychometry is an excellent exercise to flex your psychic muscles. All you need to do is to put the logical middle self aside and accept what the low self brings. It *will* be accurate.

Threads of shadowy body substance connect us with the high self. If the low self has no hindering guilt fixations, it can be trained to put out a "finger" and contact the high self, sending a flow of *vital force* along the enlarged thread to carry the thought-form of the prepared prayer. If we have correctly made prayer thought-forms with no doubts and fears ruining it, we have opened the path of communication to the high self in full faith and confidence. However, if we have not learned to reach out and touch the high self successfully in our prayer giving, all we can do is to "pray constantly"...never varying our prayer, and hope that when the high self takes our daily thoughts to use as construction material for our future, our prayer will be included without much alteration by the low self.

The reaction of the high self is automatic. (There may be more discretion here than is suspected, as observed with the firewalkers: the high self seldom fails the performer who depends on instant and constant answers to mental prayers for protection.)

The prayers themselves become unconscious, the low self having been trained to touch the high self and to present the often-used set of thought-forms of the prayer for protection. You might say this is a prayer rapport. When the hem of Jesus' garment was touched, the healing was possibly accomplished by this habitual prayer action of the low self. It is recorded that Jesus felt "the virtue go out of him" and He knew someone had been healed.

According to Huna, this "virtue" was *vital force*. The high self needs little *vital force* to use on its own level, but when it changes physical or dense materials, it needs a good force supply. This is usually taken from the individual making the prayer. The Kahunas used to order the low self to generate an extra amount of *vital force* and send it flowing up to the high self with the prayer. A healer trained in such a prayerful fashion is bound to channel a greater amount of energy to his patient. Some doctors appear to have a "healing presence," suggesting that in dedicated individuals the process may be automatic. However it flows, the energy transfusion is only as strong as the instrument through whom it is transmitted.

A common indication that contact with the high self has been made is a tingling or electrical sensation about the head, shoulders or hands because *vital force* is sent out as soon as such contact is established.

Note: *vital force* of any voltage, when used through the shadowy bodies or their protrusions appears almost intelligent in its actions, but this is not an independent action. The intelligence must be resident in the being directing the activity.

Communication with the high self occurs naturally during sleep, where dreams of the future appear frequently. Remember, only the high self can "see" into the future, so obviously there *must* be communication with the high self and the sleeper. There may be intimate contact between the high self in its shadowy body and the low self in its shadowy body, so an inspection of the stored thoughts may be made then.

It is in this nightly contact most of the thoughts are averaged by the high self and subsequently used in a mysterious mechanism to materialize corresponding events and conditions in our future. If we fear something, that fear becomes a part of our future. If we change our desires and plans frequently, our future becomes a jumble of conditions of contradiction. Psychologists now believe 98% of our ills and accidents can be traced back to origin of thought.

By building a picture of a bright future with plans of high faith, we must take care not to kick over the fragile "seed" planted by allowing ourselves a day of discouragement in which we doubt the efficacy of the practice of "holding the thought" of fruition.

Our entire lives are predicted by our thoughts. Our every thought should therefore be a prayer, for it is used by the high self as construction material for the future we envision.

It is difficult to conceive that an all-loving high self would "give" us a future of ill health or misfortune, even when we wallow in negativity. Should not the bad be cast out and only the good thoughts retained? No, we have *free will*, and as free agents, we are served the good and the bad to make our own decisions. We literally think into form

:ds of our future. Only when we correct our think-
..ıg, or ask our high self to wipe out the bad and materialize
a new and good set of thought-forms can we get assistance.
It must be noted here that an emotional heart cry of
"Help!" often reaches the high self when such communication is made in an emergency. *Emotion* automatically
activates the accumulation of *vital force*, and the high self
takes it and uses it accordingly.

Obstacles to Communication: These are complex ideas
or fixations of guilt or unworthiness, sin, doubt, fear that
the low self may stubbornly hold with its habits of
thought. A habit of thought is the result of having very
large clusters of strong old thought-forms lodged in the
memory. The moment we begin an action, mental or
physical, which calls up these habit memories, we find a
fixed set of ideas which are difficult to break down and
replace. Most of these are childhood programming, where
the sense of "sin" or guilt was instilled by well-meaning
adults. Impressed before the so-called age of reason
(seven), the low self has accepted these as fact. Thinking
itself unworthy, the low self will accept its role of prayer
communication. Or it may believe the prayer but ruin it by
the inclusion of thought-forms of doubt, fear and other
contamination.

The Kahunas called the process of clearing out the
low entity of its fixations *"clearing the path."* The path of
prayer from the low self to the high self needs some serious
reprogramming. First it must be understood that man
cannot "sin" against God or the high self. The only
recognized sin in Huna is that of hurting another. So long
as it "hurts," this sin cannot be wiped out except by
expiation.

No way can the logical middle self be convinced we
are not guilty of hurting someone unjustly; we must make
amends for the hurt. But the low self may not be convinced
even then. The unworthy fixations must be drained off.

The Huna method of draining off is similar to the
sacrifice in the early days. The low self is illogical. It can

only remember and use animal-like reasoning. It is stubborn. It can best be rid of guilt complex thought-forms by the use of physical acts or stimuli accompanied by suggestion or auto suggestion of a mild nature.

The Kahunas made certain all hurts were expiated before going on to the complexes. The patient was made to observe a fast or to do deeds of service, or give alms until it hurt. These were sacrifices. They were made with the thought of making redress for sins of ommission or commission.

The Christian practice of rites of the confessional, penance and baptism for the remission or cleansing away of sin are all duplication of ancient Kahuna practices. For example, the priest using light suggestion while sprinkling the individual with water: the holy water would act as a physical stimulus, helping to impress low self it was being cleansed of its sins. Anything will do if it is physically impressive and contains a picture of something, such as a cleansing action or a gesture of freeing. The use of physical stimulus or a series of penances which act as stimuli is very helpful in getting suggestion to take effect on the low self. Just to pray for forgiveness is usually not enough.

A test for a clear path is the test of prayer. The low self is linked with the consciousness of the middle self, feeding up memories to help furnish ideas and words with which to pray. If, therefore, when we pray there is a guilt complex in the low self, our conscience will *trouble* us, and will remain sullen and silent. When one has fasted and cleansed the low self, there is a feeling of expectancy and a joyous approach. The path is open to the heavenly Father-Mother God, the high self, and beyond.

Then the prayer may begin....

Chapter IX
Preparation
For
Prayer

The three-fold *mysteries* of Huna are the reality of the high self, and that with it man is made up of three selves. This three-self nature is of great importance, for through these channels, prayer is telepathically transmitted.

There is some reluctance on the part of some students to accept the theory prayers are sent *through* the low self to the high self (and through the high self to beings beyond, if that be necessary.) Schooled in religions in which the subconscious has had no part, and in which the low self was unknown, they believe that the conscious mind they knew was all the "soul" there is; that all that was needed was to voice a desire and it would be heard instantly by ultimate God. They balk at the role the low self must play, while admitting they are dissatisfied with answers to their prayers. This refusal to use the low self as messenger to carry the telepathic picture-message to the high self, asking as well for guidance, help and protection for the three selves, literally causes inner starvation.

The second of the three great mysteries concerns *vital force*. In the ancient sacred symbols of the Kahunas, *vital force* was represented by a grape vine. God is all life, and that life is a *living* form of force borrowed from the common store furnished by Mother Nature. It is the sunshine stored in plants used for food. Light is another symbol of this *vital force.* The worship of the sun was, to the initiates, the worship of God and of the high self. The latter was called the *True Light,* or "The *Light* that *Lighteth* each man."

The life force extracted from sunshine, air and foods by the low self was symbolized by clear water. This was the "water of life" of the ancient writings, *Mana,* in Huna.

The middle self, like the high self (both being without a physical body and digestive apparatus) must borrow its life force from the low self. The symbol for the *vital force* which it takes and uses is that of "twice powerful water" ...*Manamana* in Huna.

The high self is given the title *Lord,* which in the language of the Kahunas means "the one who supervises the division of the waters."

Vital force, when used by it, is magically strong to bring about answers to prayer. The ancient Kahunas called it *Mana loa*—the strongest life force.

The high self needs little *vital force* unless it is called upon to take a part in the life of the three selves and bring about changes in answer to prayers. Then, as the low self needs plenty of *vital force* to use when it builds a house, so it is with the high self when it undertakes to *help* build a house. In other words, when it undertakes to make changes on the dense, physical level.

We must train the low self to give some of its basic vital force to the high self whenever it delivers our prayer telepathically. This may be done daily in routine prayer or during meditation. This *vital force* is *stored* by the high self, much as a sum of money is deposited in a bank account. When a withdrawal is needed, as in any savings account, the necessary energy is there to use. The high self can then work on the dense physical level to bring about healing, to make changes in present or future conditions, or to do whatever we request in our prayers.

The third mystery has to do with the "ladder of words" so often used in the ancient writings. It is the invisible ectoplasmic (or shadowy) cord or thread along which the telepathic prayer and the *vital force* travels when sent by the low self to the high self. This is the symbol of the "beam of light" the high self represents, sometimes as a light or as the sun.

The middle self must consider very thoughtfully what it wishes to accomplish when we invite the high self to take its normal part in our daily lives. We must decide exactly what we should be and do; that it should be something worthy of the high self as well as the two lower selves. *Our goal must be to accomplish a service to humanity: it must be good and without hurt to others.*

Free will.

The Kahuna explanation of free will versus predestination is that the superconscious, the high self, or parental pair has a form of mentation or mental power unlike our own. It is above the power of recollection, characterizing the low self and above the power of inductive reason, characterizing the middle self. It is such that the high self may see that part of the future crystallized or "set." Much of the future is in a fluid or uncrystallized state, and so cannot be readily seen. Great world events seem crystallized farthest in advance. In a like way the long term events in the lives of individuals are set and may be seen, such as marriage, death, accidents or moves that affect the life-style of the individual. But even these may change, if the middle self "tears down" his wishes and desires and changes his mind about what he will do.

I have in mind a young lady who was engaged to be married. Parents and friends assumed a wedding would take place "in the foreseeable future," despite shadows of war plainly visible. Even when the couple separated, marriage was still "seen" by a number of mediums. But it never came off. The girl decided suddenly this was not what she really wanted, moved to another state and several years later married someone else.

What happened? Were all the mediums wrong? Was not her future crystallized and plainly visible? Of course. But she, by *using her free will*, chose to change that future.

Her high self literally had to tear *down* what had been projected as solidified, and gradually rebuild a future from her new thinking. Free will is our birthright. She used it to build a better future with a more stable candidate, and today affirms the wisdom of her choice.

There is a distinct philosophy in the Kahuna beliefs concerning the element of free will enjoyed by the low and the middle selves living in the human body. The high self, connected to the body by a thread of the shadowy body (through which it maintains contact) is under some compulsion to let the lower selves exercise free will and learn by experience *unless* they desire and request guidance and help from the high self. When this is requested, the high self takes a hand in the affairs of the man. Only in planning the long-term events in the life of the man is free will seemingly denied, but even then, *if proper steps are taken to change* the thinking, the events may be changed as well.

There are two kinds of free will: one for the low self in its less highly evolved state as an *animal*. The low self is under the rule of the high self, which presides over physical growth and operations connected with the body itself. Because of this direct supervision, the body conforms to definite and set patterns, while the conscious mind, or the middle self, having more complete free will, has the privilege of dictating the external activities of the body, although not its internal vital functions.

It might be said that man has two high selves, one for the low self and its guidance, and one for the middle self. The "group soul" idea of theosophy closely checks with the high self guiding the animal-man, and with the idea that the lesser animals and creatures are also guided and informed through "instincts" by the high selves watching over them in groups. As we cannot penetrate the plane of consciousness just above ours (that of the high selves), we cannot know for certain what the real state is in this relation. We can, however, observe the many acts and conditions of living things on our levels and draw a conclusion. This also holds for our observations when we see some mysterious consciousness using some mysterious force, through some mysterious form of visible matter to produce fire immunity, instant healing, prevision, the material phenomena of spiritualism, and so on.

The desirable phenomena of the seance room should be produced *without* calling on the spirits of the dead for help, and *without* the need for a medium. The circle should be used as a *source of Vital Force,* each sitter donating a little, and the leader of the group creating the thought-forms of the "prayer"—making contact with the high self, and getting its assistance (and the assistance of higher beings) in healing and helping projects.

The Huna lore of old pointed to living a normal life as the great criterion. Each living thing was thought to be in its intended stage of evolution, and there was sufficient time for everyone and everything to grow upward. Family life was good and normal in every respect. One taught or helped or healed according to his ability to work with and through his or her high self. There were no doctrines of aestheticism, no self denial. There was time and room to move forward for all, to that stage where graduation would lead to the next level of consciousness.

It can still be so, if the ancient philosophy is studied and applied. *All life is progression.* How we do it is up to us. To the Kahunas, prayer was the vital tool, a preparation of prime importance. The communication between the selves, then, "opens the path" to understanding. It is the key to the Huna philosophy.

Chapter X
Prayer

Prayer, the telepathic communication between the two lower selves and the high self is the heart of the basic system of Huna. Though prayer is a basic concept of all religions, few give the operation such a logical explanation.

God created man in his own image. Men, like God, have their creative ability, even if it be infinitesimal in comparison. God created by the use of the *"word"* by first deciding what was to be created, then by *visualizing it*, and causing it to take form. Likewise, man must decide *what* he wishes to create before he begins to pray. *Prayer is simply asking the high self to take its proper part in creating the desired conditions for which we pray, and to use its superior mental and creative abilities to help bring about desired states or conditions.*

All communication between sentient beings must be done through thoughts, or through words representing thoughts. It may also be done by thought-symbols, such as writing.

All three selves of man have their parts to play in the creative operation of prayer. If any one of the selves does not do its part, the operation is useless. And if the low self is not taught to send the prayer telepathically, after first reaching out to activate the shadowy cord to the high self, *nothing happens.*

Everything has its shadowy body, including thoughts. Thinking is done with the use of *vital force*, which works only through matter, dense or etheric. Each thought, as it is formulated, either by the low self or the middle self, or the two working in cooperation, is impressed on a microscopic portion of the substance of the low self's shadowy body. This is called a *thought-form.*

Our thoughts come in trains or clusters. Each is tied to the next by a tiny invisible thread of the same etheric substance. When we finish thinking a thought, and it passes from the focus of the conscious mind self, it is taken by the subconscious mind self and stored as memory. The storage place of these memory thought-forms is not in the physical tissues of the brain, but in the shadowy body of the low or subconscious self. When we die, the low self leaves the body in its shadowy body, and is able to take along our memories, since they are stored in the shadowy body, and therefore do not decay with the brain tissue.

When the telepathic message of thought-forms is transmitted, the sender does not give up his thought-form or "forget" it. He may be said to keep a carbon copy for his memory files. In mind reading, the mind-reader reaches out and examines the thoughts or memories of another and brings back duplicates of them; otherwise the person whose mind is read would cease to have as a memory the item read.

The reason telepathy and mind reading are rare is because both must be done by the low self. The middle self can direct the low self to send or receive a message, but cannot do it for itself. In hypnosis, the operator reaches out silently and makes contact through the use of words, in either case planting thought-forms in the low self of the subject. These may or may not be accepted by the middle self of the subject, using its reasoning mind to remain in control. In suggestology, however, the middle self, acting in its rightful role as director, issues the orders to the low self, who is bound to obey if properly trained. There is, as you see, a world of difference.

Making the Prayer

Breathe deeply, according to the heartbeat rhythm. It takes a little practice to make the heartbeat rhythm a habit and a standard way of accumulation into which you, as the middle self and the low self automatically fall as you begin the prayer action. At first the attention will be absorbed by the "count"; the command and expectation covering the accumulation of **vital force** may be neglected. But with practice, one falls into it at once and the breathing will become automatic, as the *vital force* is directed to the high self. At the same time, the prayer picture must be called to mind. Once this order has been given mentally, the picture of the *desired condition* is to be visualized as perfectly as possible. If a prayer has been memorized, it is now repeated slowly three times. The prayer may be simply a description of the desired state *as though it had already been materialized.* This description amounts in almost every case to an affirmative statement, or an affirmation. Instead of asking for health for oneself, one presents the thought-form *"seed"* picture of the end product; the finished answer to the prayer. One describes the desired state and one affirms three times ending the action with a quiet "amen" or, in the Kahuna way, "the prayer is ended," "It takes its flight" or "Let the rain of blessings fall."

The Prayer Steps

1. Once you become acquainted with your low self and have discovered its likes and dislikes, establishing a teacher-pupil relationship with love, understanding and firm discipline, your low self will know it must take orders from the middle self.

2. The low self has been taught to develop its own special talent for telepathy. It is experienced in sending thought-form clusters along the shadowy cords at the direction of the middle self.

3. The low self has been taught to accumulate a surcharge of *vital force*. If this is done by means of exercises and careful testing, a command to the low self to accumulate the surcharge is enough when comes to prayer time.

   Preparation review:

1. Amends must be made for hurt done to

others. Or, if this cannot be done directly, good deeds, gifts to charity and fasting will help convince your low self (as well as the middle self) that the books have been balanced, and that one is now deserving of help from the high self.

2. *Know what you want!* Make sure you add "for the good of all concerned, and of hurt to no one." Project yourself into the future and imagine yourself living the new condition. Make very sure the low self is in full agreement that the desired condition is truly desirable and worth the work necessary to bring it about. Accept also the *responsibility* of granting the request which may come about.

3. The plan will be made for a series of daily prayers on the same subject, always formulating the prayer in exactly the same way. *Do write it out and recite it as an affirmation three times daily.*

4. Three or four unrelated things should not be presented in the same prayer action. It is best to present each one in a separate prayer, spaced at least an hour apart, after practicing a vivid visualization of each one in turn.

5. Visualize the end results which are desired, and do not be too specific as to *how* they should be brought about. This leaves the high self free to bring about the desired condition in its own way. Your high self cannot be forced or commanded to do what would be the wrong thing, by answering a prayer for something that would bring the wrong conditions to anyone. Ask of the Father that the prayer be accepted and acted upon, always with the proviso that it is something good and fitting and proper to be brought about.

6. Take time to practice long enough so that a

swift and easy contact can be made with the high self at any time, even though a prayer is not made. Such practice is simple. There should first be an accumulation of surplus of *vital force*, then a quieting down and meditating on the nature of the high self, the fact that it is variable, and that it is always waiting, willing and eager to be asked to take its full part in the job of living the happy, successful and helpful life.

The love of the high self is always with us, and our love for our high self should always be the central theme in every meditation. Remember, one must arouse an emotional response of love in the low self, a response which can be felt and shared by the conscious self. *This love is the magnetic force which draws the low self to make the contact with the high self, and to desire to make its gift to it in the form of a sending of vital force across the shadowy cord of connection.*

Love ever desires to give and to serve and the ideal gift from the lower man to the high self is *vital force.* Such a gift, given freely, and without a prayer attached to the giving, is the ideal offering. It makes it possible for the high self to bring about such things on the physical level of life as one may desire to help accomplish. Through your high self one can, with such gifts, help to bring needed assistance to others, even to serve on a world scale.

Instant or miraculous answers require a very large amount of *vital force* to enable the high self to bring about the changes required on the physical plane. Only an exceptional individual will be able to accumulate a sufficient *vital force* surcharge and offer it with a sufficiently well-made picture of the desired conditions for instant answers. *Some problems, especially those involving the lives of others, take additional time to work out through a gradual change in circumstances.*

Steps to be Taken in Making the Huna Prayer for Instant Healing Fire Immunity or Change in the Future

1. The low self must be trained to put out a "finger" of its shadowy body and follow the invisible threads which will guide it to the high self.
2. It must be trained to send thought-forms along the paths of contact, as in telepathy and mind reading.
3. It should be trained to generate an extra supply of *vital force on command*, then to send it along the paths of contact as needed.
4. If contact with the high self is not made, the path must be cleared by removing the guilt complexes from the low self.
5. The prayer must be most carefully made, after due consideration of possible unexpected consequences, should the prayer be answered. When the final decisions are reached as to what is desired, the prayer is to be formed by working it aloud three times over, using the *will* to impress the prayer on the low self and to build strong concentration of thought-form clusters.
6. It is suggested that the prayer be *written out* in detail.
7. The prayer when thus made is held in mind and the low self ordered to reach out and to touch the high self. When an answering electrical tingle is felt, the prayer is recalled (or even spoken aloud) again, so that it can be sent to the high self with the extra supply of *vital force* needed to materialize the thought-forms of the prayer into immediate or future events.

If prayer is made for the healing or help of another, this individual must be cleansed of all guilt complexes as a preliminary act, otherwise his low self will prevent the fruition of the act.

Prayer Review

Bring the picture of the thing to be prayed for *clearly*

to mind. Nothing must be added or taken awa
after the first prayer of any series is made, unless
self is asked to drop the entire prayer and begin a   . ᴜʟ
some good reason.

*Faith must be reaffirmed if anything has come up to
weaken it between sessions of prayer.* A strong affirmation of
faith is often needed each day before the prayer begins.

Tell no one of your prayer or its contents!

The surcharge of *vital force* is accumulated and the
low self is told to hold it ready for the moment when
contact is made with the high self and the gift of *vital force*
can be made.

Sufficient meditation on the high self is made (relax
the body and assume a comfortable position,) to arouse
the emotion of love for the high self in the low self. Having
learned that the reason for meditation is to focus the
thoughts and to allow it to make its contact with the high
self, the low self will soon learn to respond with love, to
make that contact at once as well as to start sending the gift
of *vital force* for that particular moment of prayer. A rush
of emotion and love may engulf the selves at this point as
the three selves respond to one another in perfect unison.
The presence of the high self may be felt by electrical
sensations in the physical body.

Once the contact with the high self is recognized, the
low self is asked to send the prayer picture (thought-form
clusters) on a flow of additional *vital force* by the telepathic
communion.

The Kahunas made it a practice to voice their prayer
by describing the desired condition while recalling it
clearly and vividly to mind. They memorized the short
description, word for word, and recited it three times, as a
means of strengthening the "seed" while sending the *vital
force* to "water" it. (The memorization of the description,
after writing it out with thought and care, will have
impressed the prayer picture on the low self very strongly
and clearly.)

When the picture has been described aloud or in

silence, the prayer is ended with the same purpose and precision as it was begun. Simply say "I give thanks, loving Father, and now leave the prayer picture in Your hands to build into physical reality in the future, just as it is already a reality on Your level of being. Let the rain of blessings in the form of high *vital force* fall. I now withdraw from contact."

The prayer, once made, is to be released into the keeping of the high self until next time contact is made and fresh *vital force* is to be offered, together with a restatement or additional strengthening layer for the original seed picture.

Avoid hurried prayers. If prayer is to be effective, it must be made in an orderly fashion and with eagerness, drive and a strongly awakened and moving love. It is the will of the middle self which directs and controls the work, and this force is not exerted unless the conscious self is alert and is concentrating its full attention as it directs each step and supervises the low self in the part it is to play.

Leave your worries behind! Faith must be reaffirmed and serenity reached for the meditation approach. Once one has learned to make easy prayer contact with the high self, one may find it well to make the *vital force* gift, then to affirm that this worry or that is laid aside completely. After the letting go of such worries, one then may make a simple verbal request, (depending on the low self to send the thought-forms of the request to the high self) such as "Father, I have put away this thing which has bothered me. I now ask that you forgive and cleanse it away." This easily cleanses the low and the middle self, and may be done at any time, whether a full prayer is to follow or not.

Suggestions for Certain Prayers
Prayer to High Self for Help and Protection
We ask that our high self guard, guide and instruct *us* according to its superior mentation in every challenge facing *us* this day/night.

For Others

We ask that *our* high self reach out to the high self of (name), that the path may be cleared and open, and that whatever is needed will be directed to this dear one, tempered to his/her spiritual development *for the good of all concerned.*

Prayer of Thanks

We thank *our* high self for our blessings of health, blessings of wealth, blessings of love, blessings of success and blessings of peace of mind. Amen.

Thanks for blessings received is most important to both the high self and the low self. Appreciation should be as automatic as a call for help. Nothing unites the *selves* as completely as a mutual feeling of love and well-being.

Think of the prayer and the desired outcome *as something already as real as the plant in the seed.* The difference is in the time that must be given for the growth, not in the basic reality. Understanding this, one can think of the desired condition as being already a reality without insulting one's reasoning powers or intelligence.

Do all you can to bring your prayer about. Whatever will impress *your* low self, act out the part.

When I completed my novel *Angel in the Rigging* and eagerly alerted the publishing world, I took a book from the shelf in my office and dressed it up in a crisp white cover. I printed the title across the top with my name, the publisher and his location at the bottom. *I visualized my book in published form.*

The three selves are partners in living, and each partner must do his utmost to bring about desired conditions.

Prayer is an act of creation, in which all three selves play their allotted parts.

Chapter XI
Outlaw
Memories

What if all instructions for prayer or healing are faithfully followed — and nothing happens? Is the "system" at fault? Or is it the practitioner?

Let's look at your *understanding* of sin, amends, atonement, purification, prayer for forgiveness, etc. Now consider the Huna concept of sin. Does it relate to the "law" proclaimed by some prophet? Not really. The Polynesian interpretation of sin goes far deeper, wider and broader. *It is anything that is bad for the human being or his fellows.* This means to hurt others mentally and emotionally. It is something that prevents the low self from contacting the high self along the shadowy cord and delivering the prayer (blocking the path). It breaks up the triunity. In other words, if the act causes an individual to be cut off by his low self from his high self, a sin is committed.

In the translation of their ancient words, the Kahunas used the symbol of the spider's web with flies caught in it. Each fly was a memory, and all flies were connected by the strands of the web with all other flies. In the center lay the spider—the man made of his low self and his middle self—aware of the presence of each fly and able to run out to inspect it any time. The thin strands of the web stood for the shadowy thread, and the normal memory was one tied to all other memories in a *rationalization* process as it was made, thought through and considered.

A memory stored *without* being rationalized is sometimes stored in the low self. This set of thought-forms will not be tied in correctly with other thought forms, and because the middle self did not do its part and rationalize the memory made, the middle self never has that particular memory given back to it as one recalled. It is an outlaw memory. The low self knows it is not normal and is ashamed or afraid of it. The low self will then harbor a sense of guilt because of bad deeds done by the low and the middle selves, *and will not face high self across the shadowy cord.* In exactly the same way, the low self will not face the middle self when such unrationalized memories weigh it down. It tries to rationalize them in its illogical fashion. As a result the middle self can recall none of these memories and will automatically react to certain events connected with these outlaws in strange ways: flying into a rage; being filled with unreasonable fear or some other emotion welling up from deep within. He may not be able to think normally when such outlaw memories come up. He may find a blank in his memory, even amnesia. He may think friends are enemies; feel himself superior to others; react physically in jerking, trembling motions; become hysterical, paralyzed, blind, deaf or dumb for a short time. He may produce "ailments" no physician can find, reacting mentally, physically and emotionally because there is tied up with each memory cluster something that gauges the amount of *vital force* used automatically which literally explodes when that particular memory cluster is activated by circumstance.

Normally most memories arouse little emotion within the low self, so use little *vital force*. Emotions use up *vital force* faster than anything else. Thus, middle self is deprived of its share of *vital force*, and is entangled in psychotic or neurotic emotions it cannot control.

Symbols used by the Kahunas to indicate that which cuts one off from the high self abound in sacred (and profane) literature: thorns and thistles; the dragon or serpent and any wild beast, particularly a lion, are some examples given.

A snare, made of a thread, cord or rope, is symbolic of the shadowy threads and the tangle of the outlaw memories (*sins*) which tempt or capture one or otherwise hold us captive. A stumbling block of any kind is also used frequently; so is a cross in any shape.

All these symbolize the fixations and obsessions, the outlaws that trip us. They will block the path, or the way, or the road. A straight path or stretched cord is the symbol of the opened path; a crooked path or tangled cord is the symbol of the shadowy cord which is entirely or partially blocked. On such a path the low self will rarely send a prayer to the high self on the command of the middle self. *It must be cleared.*

The Kahunas used a wooden cross in the form of an X on the path leading to the temple. It was the sign of taboo in Huna. It was placed on the path as a warning that the uncleansed must not proceed. The temple, of course, symbolized the "place of the most High."

Dust, seeds, or fine particles represented the thought-forms. The word Huna means "fine dust particles" showing how important the Kahunas considered the understanding of thought-forms. These are symbolized as acting in clusters, the "seeds" of the prayer, and forming other clusters in the outlaw and unrationalized memories cutting man off from his high self.

Normally fixations are mild and can be discovered by self-analysis or with the help of a friend, and the path thus made clear. In extreme cases a doctor or psychoanalyst may be consulted. Of course the physical well being of the self must be considered. Where there is disease or disturbance of any kind, a competent physician should be consulted.

The Kahunas recognized one other fixation: that mental and physical ills can also come from spirit influence. In Huna, these are spirits which attach themselves to the living, and to a great extent, live on the *vital force* of the individual. They are able to inject their own thoughts at times into the consciousness of the low self, and even more often their emotions or moods. Modern psychiatry refers to such fixations as "split-off" parts of personality. The Kahunas believed and taught that the high self can remove even the most powerful of the obsessing entities. The supply of *vital force* must be diverted from the evil spirits by ceasing to respond to their urges. This is something the middle self must cause the low self to handle and involves a complete conversion and change of the way of life from evil to good. Outside help is always recommended for the cleansing of these fixations and prayerful help. When these are removed, the path can be opened.

For a normal blockage of prayer, the middle self simply talks things over with the low self in the meditative state. Once you have control of the low self (and know what your animal is), it is a matter of elimination. The low self may be hung up over a childhood incident taken too seriously. We are programmed as children by well meaning adults. Examine these memories in the light of your own maturity. If they are immature and unreasonable, discard them. Put a new set of ideas into your computer. Convince your low self you ar worthy of that for which you are praying: repeat and repeat!

The low self may be simply lazy. It may not want to make the effort to help the middle self in its desires. An extreme example would be a complete lack of interest in life. Sometimes memories of former experiences of unsuccessful efforts for accomplishment cause a breakdown in communication between the two selves.

One called to mind is that of a divorcee making vain efforts to recoup her marriage after she had instigated the divorce proceedings herself. When the former partner clearly indicated no further interest in her, she suffered a severe depression and withdrew from family, friends and all social contact, letting it even affect her work.

Another concerned a brilliant young composer who could not get his work published. In a fit of despondency, he threw everything into a trunk, stopped composing, and today is a sad object of bottle-fatigue.

In both cases, the low self was definitely out of control, and the middle self was letting him get away with it, in clear violation of the middle self's responsibilities. The middle self must *always* be in control and is directly responsible for the low self at all times.

When this happens, desire has to be aroused once more, with an element of ambition, and sufficient renewal of confidence and faith in the high self and God to go ahead and make fresh tries—or to build a new life.

Old habits, hates and grudges are common offenders of a blocked path. A chronically ill woman went from doctor to doctor with no relief for headaches that became more intense with the years. Finally a wise old practictioner who had known the family for years told her bluntly to go home and make peace with her daughter-in-law. Though highly incensed, she hurt badly enough to give the matter a trial. Within a week of the reconciliation she was free from pain.

There are even cases of individuals refusing healing prayers. They fear the loss of the care and solicitude from family and friends, as well as the prospect of shouldering responsibilities again evaded by the current illness. Their low self is saying clearly: *"Leave me alone! I'm where I am because I want to be here."* Leave them their free will.

The low selves in the examples cited above all need a complete working over to break down and correct old belief habits. As a rule the middle self cannot do this for himself, and outside help is definitely recommended, be it a sympathetic and understanding friend or a professional analyst. The Kahunas were both.

Religious beliefs of earlier training frequently cause fixations, especially where people are told to interpret the Bible literally and without question. The low self is impressed by the printed word, and they have been told the Bible is the law of God.

It is, to a degree. But how that law has been interpreted is another matter. Researchers have theorized for hundreds of years a coded symbology is contained in all sacred script, not only to protect it from the uninitiated but to protect man before he is able to understand the teachings.

This is the mind age, when the search for truth has had more light shed on it than in several previous centuries. The light is Huna, and may well be one of the most exciting discoveries of this age.

Those who claim they have never had success in prayer work at all had better take a good look at themselves. They could be blocked by greed or intolerance they refuse to acknowledge, and would be deeply offended were it called to their attention. These concern not only intolerances against other nationalities, races and creeds, but judgments against class and social customs and bias against sex and living conditions.

Jesus taught there must be love and mercy in our dealings with others and even our thoughts of them. Any attitude of mind denying compassion to others is almost certain to be accompanied by a sense of guilt or unworthiness in the low self, even if hidden from sight. We have all had grounding in fair play and common decency. Where the conscious mind flouts it, there will be conflict with the low self because such training is deeply ingrained with our earliest memories.

The matter of making amends for hurts done to others was a basic part of the Kahuna methods for clearing the path. Why is obvious when the low self reactions are studied. An irritable word spoken in haste is remembered by the low self, and will not be cancelled out until apologies erasing the hurt inflicted are made. It is not always necessary to make apology to the person offended directly. Simply reach out to him in the meditative state and ask for forgiveness. Or, if you feel this is not enough, giving to a good cause (until it hurts) is another way to appease the low self.

If the low self feels a punishment is due for past deeds

of hurt, physical stimulus may be used by penance, such as fasting, or denying oneself pleasurable habits for a prescribed time. Volunteer work may also be done, impressing the low self that both time and money are expended as an additional offering.

One of the great teachings of Jesus (reflected also in the Huna philosophy) was that direct atonement to one formerly injured could be balanced by several good deeds done in restitution. "Inasmuch as ye have done it unto the least of these, my brethren, ye have done it unto me." This means if you cannot make amends to the person hurt directly, good deeds may be substituted, or done to others as payment in kind.

Habits of thoughts are very strong. The low self is hard to grasp and force into new lines of thought and action. When working on one of these, I write out affirmations to that effect and put them around the house where they are seen frequently. Your eyes are cameras. *Take a picture of the changes you wish to make.* The low self will get the picture, and bring forth memories of the past of things and conditions long forgotten. The older the fixations, the further back they are buried in your memory banks. They may no longer matter to the middle self, but the low self still remembers old hopes, fears, ambitions, affronts and desires. As you houseclean these old memories, you will feel a greater peace of mind. Gradually you will find yourself praying with more sensation of contact with the high self.

Then, as normal relations between the three selves are established, the high self may once more draw the *vital force* from the low self, effecting corrections and healing in body, mind and soul.

Then you will be attuned to the infinite.

Chapter XII
Meditation

The Kahunas believed it was only possible to contact the *Aumakua* (parental high self) when one had freed and cleared his mind of all negativity. It was necessary to relax the body, the emotions and the mind. The body must be made to lose all tensions and be free of any strains that might interfere with the thinking process. The mind must also be relaxed, so that it can be open to psychic impressions. Most important is the relaxation of the emotions. If there is envy, hate, or some other negative emotion, it must be cleared from the mind before the higher positive forces can be put to work. Breathe to the count of the heart rhythm.

When the mind is empty, it appears the head is filled with light. This is the inner light of the psychic sight. The Kahunas believed that psychic light entered from the back of the head, filling the inner cavern of the haven of the spirit. The consciousness must then be focused on the purpose of meditation.

If there is a problem, think of it as if God and the high self were solving it. Feel that the problem is already solved, and be receptive to the solution. Deepen your breathing.

When you are sending someone healing energy, close your eyes and *see* the person in your mind's eye. Then picture him cured from the physical or emotional disease.

These steps are simple, but vital in successful meditation. Use prayers and affirmations most meaningful to *you*. Nothing should disturb you. It may take time.

As you practice daily you will find yourself gradually going deeper with no necessity for counting consciously. You will see flashes of lights and colors.

Faces and forms will come and go; flowers and birds, even shapeless nonentities will flash upon your vision. You may hear sounds and smell odors and feel the touch of invisible hands. You need not wonder at or fear the sights and sounds of the astral realm—nor consider their entertainment. Gradually you will go into yet deeper levels with full conscious awareness that you are in control of all your faculties (the low self). Here, at the deepest level, you will make the contact with your high self. Here you will receive the answers to your everyday challenges. This is known as "going within" where the contact with your innermost being can be made.

Sincere prayer and meditation is done without doubt or pretension. Here is the healing level, the level that reveals the future. You pass beyond mind to the great power of the universe.

When you fill your mind with positive power, the lower force of emotions will vanish. The Hawaiians believed man is the child of the gods and could communicate with them at will. So can you with *faith, trust and honest prayer.* This is where all the answers are—*within, in communication with your own high self.*

". . . be still and know that I *am* God."

Chapter XIII
The Huna
Approach
To Dreams

Dreams are the open door to the past as well as to the future. We dream in symbols, often pictured in strange settings that make little sense to the logical mind. Dreams should never be taken literally. They should be thoughtfully studied, analyzed and interpreted *by ourselves.*

The Kahunas believed dream interpretation could furnish man an understanding of his destiny. They taught that when the body is asleep, the *Aumakua* high self maintains its vigil and infuses or implants dreams in the mind of the low self. These dreams may be of instruction, of warning or precognition. In sleep, the high self collects the thoughts projected by the low and the middle self and with these fashions the blueprint for the individual's future. When the sleeper has put himself into jeopardy with his thinking, his high self steps in and warns him of the consequence. These warnings man may accept or reject, for he has free will.

The low self changes memories of thoughts or impressions of events, translating them in dreams into terms of visual impressions. It will often "scramble" the picture with images familiar to it, joining one idea to another through a process of association, thus making a symbol personal to the dreamer. A cooperative low self will bring the middle self symbols he can understand.

We are all unique. Each of us must find his own potential and develop it. A person who uses his potential progresses. When you value the best within yourself, you will value the best in others. If you cannot love yourself, you cannot love others. *We must grow or self destruct.* Only by realizing and working *with* the God within himself can mankind reach his ultimate goal: graduation to the next level beyond.

Symbols are extremely personal, and therefore mean something different to each dreamer. Only *you* yourself can know and understand what your dreams are telling you, for only you know your own secret thoughts and action.

What is the stuff dreams are made of? Bits and pieces of your personal life, hobbies, activities, reading, viewing and of course the professional climate in which you move daily.

A nurse, a laboratory technician and a physician, for example would dream symbols pertaining to the medical world, clinical situations and also the tools of that profession.

Those moving in the business world, on the other hand, outpicture the financial world, business transactions and the tools and machinery of that activity.

The symbology used by one in the creative field is oddly similar, no matter what area the dreamer moves. These people move in the highly imaginative realms where creativity blooms and project a strong mystic aura whether awake or asleep.

The dreamer who does hard physical labor uses dreams as an escape or to rest his aching body. This is not to say their dreams are not of creative intensity. A dockworker who paints seascapes in his spare time has a wider interest range than the artist locked up in a studio painting only from "inspiration." Our postman wrote beautiful poetry while walking his route. Undoubtedly his dream symbols were full of flights of fancy and gentle imagery. A bus driver who scribbled on his novel during his "waiting" period had, I'm sure, more than transportation and traffic symbols in his dreams. Personal habits as well as our reaction to other people has an important bearing on our dream results.

What about dreaming of well known sports figures or television personalities? One young man posed this question when asking for help in interpreting his nocturnal experiences. My answer was phrased in a question. "What does that sports figure or television personality mean to *you?*"

He was an avowed water sports enthusiast, it was discovered. The Olympic gold-medal winner Mark Spitz, appearing in several dreams, could represent health, discipline or even speed. But since the dreamer also participated in competitive sports, here was the key. Spitz represented an aspect of the dreamer, the ambition or goal. The details of the dream also pointed up the health and clean-living necessary to maintain championship participation—a rule the dreamer was not living. He saw very quickly what his dream was telling him. That one symbol set the stage for the entire drama. Though accepting the validity of the dream warning, he chose not to give up his partying and nonathletic sports. At last report he was not doing too well in his own competition.

Universal symbols are those representing the same image in many cultures and civilizations, such as nature, food, shelter, clothing, transportation, etc. Religious symbols, thought the creeds vary, are also surprisingly similar. National symbols are pretty well taken for granted and easily recognized. The bald eagle, for example, is the American national bird. The lion represents the United Kingdom. The bear symbolizes Russia. Uniforms of any kind almost always represent a higher authority in the line of some discipline. Even the high self, the middle self and the low self find their way into your dreams, and you may recognize them as easily as did one young lady who saw "a very beautiful lady with long dark hair every time I was tempted to run with a certain crowd at college. She never said anything to me, just stood there and looked at me. I could still see her dark, compelling eyes, even after I woke up! As soon as I straightened myself out, the dream stopped. I have no idea who she is—"

Really? Ask your low self. I'm sure the answer will be prompt. The high self is watching.

Artistic people who spend more time in the creative meditative state than most people often have ideas "just come out of the blue." A woman who paints exquisite portraits admits she "sees" the colors in her dreams long before they can be translated on the canvas. She often "meets" the people in her dreams before she is commissioned to paint a portrait of them.

How does this happen? She expects it to be so, and it is. Writers confess this oftens happens to them. Characters will write themselves into their productions. Often names, titles and whole plots appear first in the dream of novelists. Adela Rogers St. John admits this freely. So do many others. My own experience was unique because of the time element.

About fifteen years ago I dreamed I was in a large city, observing a rush-hour crowd emerging from a subway. Everyone was wearing conventional dress, but on the shoulder of every individual was an *animal head*.

My first reaction on waking was this would make a good story—but how, or why did not follow. The dream was repeated two more times; then stopped. I thought about it for a long time, wondering if I had dreamed a plot of a book already published (or a motion picture produced), but no one had ever heard of it before. The librarian, with her bibliographic computer mind assured me no such story existed and suggested I write it myself. But nothing would gel.

Some years later I became acquainted with Huna, and suddenly the dream made sense. It came again, just as dreamed before—and this time I recognized the people in my dream, but they were none I knew in my daily life. Then the meaning came clear. They were characters in a book, and as quickly the plot fell into place. The *Carnal Connection* almost wrote itself.

The interpretation of dreams may at first appear difficult. This need not be so, once you understand *how* and where the symbols come from: your own notes. Keep a record of your dreams. Jot down everything that comes on waking, then transform it later to a more permanent record. There is a reason for doing this. Often you have little time in the morning to do more than make sporadic notes. Do this if you wake up at night, even if it means keeping a flashlight by the bedside or writing in the dark. *The low self will be impressed* and bring more when you show your determination to put it to work, for it is the low self that brings the dreams to the conscious mind. Note the time. Note also the emotion felt in the dream or on waking. Soon you will note certain symbols will occur frequently, and these are your springboard. Review your dreams weekly.

The Kahunas believe that a direct "seeing" of a future event may be passed on to us by the low self. Sometimes the low self mixes what it sees or senses with things already known to it, thus producing a symbol which the middle self will understand. A perceptive middle self will "sense" the mood of the low self, for such emotions frequently set the stage for the entire dream drama. Interpreting dreams through Huna is an easy thing to do because you, as the middle self, direct the low self before going to sleep that a dream *will be* recalled. Sometimes the low self plays games and refuses to cooperate. This is where training the low self is very important. Remind the low self you are in a partnership, working out your mutual salvation. Pavlov's method is an excellent one: do use the reward system, but use some common sense. If your low self has a weight challenge, do not reward it with a chocolate fudge sundae.

Like any animal, the low self reacts to praise, love and endless patience.

For your permanent record, a simple guide is suggested, but please do not feel this is a firm outline. Be relaxed with your dreams and work out whatever feels comfortable to you.

Dream details	Interpretation
1. Setting. (background)	1.
2. Situation (action and reaction)	2.
3. People, animals, objects, etc.	3.
4. Emotional tone registered: fear, love, etc.	4.
5. "Feeling" of message	5.
6. When dream occurred. (time of night)	6.
7. Other information given.	7.

Write down any psychic impressions you may get when recording your dream (7). This is most important. This nearly always ties in with something that happened the previous day or week. It may well have been on your mind before going to sleep, and went out (subconsciously), as a mental prayer for help.

A woman in charge of an anniversary birthday dinner celebration made reservations at a local hotel for sixty guests. A week before the event only twenty-four reservations had been paid. With grave concern she called on her high self for help. In a dream, her son told her a surprise birthday party was in progress for his sister, and he asked the mother to take the daughter shopping upstairs until a certain hour, then to meet him on the seventh floor.

When they stepped off the elevator, a large crowd, all wearing formal attire, swelled the lobby, crying out

even though the dress and mode of living differed from my provincial upbringing, *had happened to me* in some vague past. I know now that it was a flashback to a lifetime when the catacombs were used for living, burial, and in some instances, incarceration.

Briefly, I was locked up in an underground room. In time, the soldiers would come to get me and I would be killed. In my dream I was taken to the room by a stern white haired man with a flowing white beard. It was small, with a high ceiling, and no opening except for the door. Footsteps sounded, and I 'knew' the soldiers were coming. Cold, sheer terror shook me as I frantically tried to find a way of escaping. The door opened—and I wakened. Never did the dream go any further. Mercifully, perhaps, the memory was cut off.

But the emotion was still locked in my subconscious, and this *had to be removed* from the low self's storage, or, at best, neutralized. Common sense of course will tell us that we cannot go back and re-live another lifetime. *But we can change the emotion by rewriting the script.*

I do not, of course, recall praying for help as such, but surely the middle self was disturbed enough to send a plea to the high self for release. Something told me I had to dream myself out of that situation, and then everything would be peaceful.

So I did. Step by step the dream was recalled. Then, as soon as I was locked in the cell, I looked up and *visualized a high window* in my prison. Before the steps echoed down the corridor, I was pulling myself up and *out*—then, even as the door opened behind me, I escaped to safety.

Interestingly, as soon as this was done, the dream vanished completely and I was able to sleep again. The high self *does* guide and help us *when we ask for its participation*, when we desire help.

Some dreams are no more than images floating across the consciousness when one is falling asleep. Waking visions do take place, but they are rare. Experiences in deep meditation are the rewards of dedicated practice and occur when we least expect them. On more than one occasion I not only heard but saw fully materialized both my female high self and my male high self. The woman frequently brought a delightful floral fragrance. The man's touch was evident on numerous occasions. These are indescribable experiences one can only appreciate when they are a personal happening.

There are dreams that are reveries coming from very strong impressions on the mind during waking hours reappearing during the sleep cycle. These are also unusual, but delightfully valid.

Bear in mind that dreams appearing just before waking in the morning are precognitive and should be noted carefully for special messages and guidance. They are the high self talking ot the low self and the middle self, reflecting your waking thinking. Here you are offered a blueprint of your future. If you do not like what you have built up for yourself, *change your thinking and your future will be altered accordingly.*

The aware middle self working with the high self can make serious changes when so forewarned, frequently avoiding an impending disaster. The stories of passengers changing a flight that later crashed; changes in railroad accomodations after a warning dream are numerous. Such warnings came to many passengers of the ill-fated *Titanic,* the *Lusitania* as well as the later *Andrea Doria;* some heeded them, others did not. The high self only advises. Free will is man's perogative. *How* you live your life is up to you.

How do you change a future dream event to a condition for the better? *Is it really possible?* Many students of Huna keeping dream records claim they have done so and lived the changes made. This is getting the selves working together in harmony for the good of all concerned. Examples always tell the story best:

The dream was short and to the point. I was looking

for a three-shelf book case and found myself in an otherwise empty room of a large house. The furniture was constructed of new wood, newly sanded and ready to stain or paint, and in a sturdy condition. A voice said "You can have everything *on the book case*, should you desire to purchase it." Thinking some books went with the deal, I looked closer and found only a paperweight on the top shelf. Picking it up to examine it, I found it was very heavy but beautifully detailed in old bronze. Delighted with my bonus, I was about to finalize the sale when a second examination revealed the object was a coiled snake with a kite-shaped head with green-jade eyes. Putting it down quickly, I indicated I wanted the bookshelf only, waking up with a feeling of revulsion and cold dread.

Snakes, as such do not bother me, for research has taught me they represent the ancient symbol of wisdom and the *vital force* in Huna. Why, then, the emotional reaction on waking?

Putting myself back into the dream, I changed the object on the shelf. What is the opposite to a snake? I could only think of a crucifix, because my low self recognized the spiritual symbol of Christianity as such, and the serpent as evil. When my imagination completed it, the crucifix was a beautiful cross encrusted with precious stones. Placing it on top of the bookshelf, I claimed it, and woke with a feeling of deep inner peace. This is important. *Do* change the emotion dreamed as well. You will find out why later.

Not long afterwards I was in a situation where an acquaintance publicly projected such hate and negativity towards me, my sensitive low self flipped his tail and demanded we stalk from the room. Taking a deep breath, I mentally called for the high self's assistance, and was immediately impressed to bombard my assailant with a volley of love and blessings. In other words, the negativity was returned with love, polarizing or neutralizing it.

Interestingly enough, such action affects both parties.

Not fifteen minutes later the antagonist came over and greeted me with a complete change of attitude, much to the astonishment of several spectators taking in the entire scene. (All commented later they could see the assailant's expression change from puzzled harshness to softness before their eyes.) Before the evening was over all was amicable, the atmosphere cleared.

What really happened?

By projecting love, hate was neutralized. As my own thinking changed, so did the thinking of my opponent. It changed as well the feelings of all in that room, changing the vibrations to a more comfortable atmosphere for everyone present.

Not until I was on the way home did the realization dawn as the previous dream flashed to mind. *I had lived the change made!* What a beautiful reality! By using the same tools, anyone can do the same. What will it be, the snake or the crucifix?

When interpreting a dream, simply *let the mind go.* Consider all the possible meanings of the dream, and suddenly the idea will come to mind at will. Daily practice is most important. It will help to bring some clairvoyance into focus in which distant scenes may be observed. Visions within the storage of the low self may rise. When the middle self and the low self cooperate, the high self will shower them with blessings, reaching down to the low self before the call is even made, reminding us of the Biblical promise:

"Before ye ask it shall be given unto you."

The importance of recording your dream cannot be overstressed. The low self has a way of forgetting details, no matter how good our memory may be. On the other hand, the physical act of writing something down impresses the low self, who is always eager to play a starring role in any drama. Often while writing down some fragment of a dream, others will flash into mind or even forgotten details from fragments remembered.

If you have not dreamed for a long period of time, have a talk with your low self and impress it with the importance of this communication. Eventually, something *will* be forthcoming. Write it down at *once*, even if you must do so in the dark. Sometimes I find notes on my bedside pad I have not the slightest recollection recording. As soon as possible write your jottings down in a permanent form, and as you do so, fill in the blank spaces by using your notes. After all, these are *your* thoughts and *your* dreams. *You* are shaping your future. All depends on *your* selves and how much attuned they are to each other. Only under *your* direction can they communicate to become a "whole I!"

The Kahuna ability to "change the future" for others by those requesting this service is best explained by the reminder that these adepts were psychics in tune with their high self through long years of training and practice. They could "read" the thought-pattern of the person requesting this information, and could ascertain to what extent that pattern was solidified, gauging as well the condition of that individual. Only after careful meditation and study would permission be given.

The guilt complexes of the personality were studied, and after a certain ritual, removed. Penance, similar to the confessional of Catholics, was given. Note, in both instances, the priest is impressing the low self with the awareness that some sacrifice must be made before a change can be effected. An admonition is issued, which would direct a change of attitude. The high self of the Kahuna, with the cooperation of the high self of the person seeking help, tears down the thought pattern, and a new thought pattern is laid out for a new future.

Briefly, then, the middle self "makes the picture" of a desired condition, gives it to the low self who in turn takes it to the high self. The high self, in cooperation with other high selves (the *Poe Aumakua* of the Polynesians, or company of high selves) performs the actual work.

In the ancient lore, the kingdom of God (heaven) is the high self symbolized as a higher plane. In a like manner, the kingdom of earth is occupied by the low self with its companion middle self. To "seek the kingdom of God" then, is to learn that there *is* a high self and to accept that it is willing and able to come to our assistance. This means also to accept the low self's role in the triunity, which is to contact the high self by means of the shadowy thread, and to present the *vital force* and the prayer. Only when you learn to contact your high self can the prayers be delivered, and all things be given accordingly.

Jesus, the Nazarene Kahuna said it well.

"It is not I that doeth the work, but the Father within me."

Go thou and do likewise.

Chapter XIV
Your
Heart's
Desire

In Volume IV of the Masters, Spalding says whenever the Hawaiians go out in their canoes they take along at least one man in each canoe who is a "living" compass. The concern of the others is to work the boats; his business is to pilot at all times. *They have brought this capacity down through the ages with them.*

So ingrained are some of the "old ways," even modern Hawaiians, who have had no training in Huna follow the path of the high self automatically, a little astonished that everything just "seems to fall into place."

A neighbor of pure Hawaiian ancestry confessed when I was searching for material for a book that she was ignorant of her heritage. The family had lived in Honolulu for three generations, had been educated in the western fashion, attended a Christian church and had no interest in the past. Yet, she has an uncanny *knowing* whenever one of her children is in trouble and contacts them *even before the trouble has manifested.* She lives a life of service and gives freely to anyone in need. *She is living the old way,* though unaware of it.

The high self stands ever by to assist, when invited to share the living of the lower selves, even when that invitation is unconsciously felt. That invitation is clearly given in Matthew 7:7: *"Ask, and it shall be given to you: seek, and you shall find: knock and it shall be opened to you."*

You may well ask: Is there a specific formula that I may follow to receive my dearest wish? The steps are defined in the chapter on *prayer* and should be reviewed each time a request is made. Huna is an ancient philosophy. *It is basic. It is simple.* It survived to this day because it is also adaptable. It has come through countless cultures and many civilizations. It may be adopted with confidence, even in this computer age. Let us therefore "program" a specific request by "feeding" into our computer (brain) exactly what is wanted, according to the Huna method.

We will take a hypothetical personality and call him John. He wants a better job and has his eye on an opening coming up within the company where he works. He feels he is qualified and deserving.

First, let's learn something about John. He is single, age 26, graduate of a business college, and employed as head teller of a large branch of a state-wide bank, with whom he has been for the past three years. He has a four year old car, lives in a modest one bedroom apartment close to work and has been seriously dating Mary, a second grade school teacher in her second year of teaching. The new job would mean marriage and downpayment on a condominium. John has ambitions to move up in the banking world and has already taken the management trainee schooling. *How does he go about his programming?*

Note, first of all, John has already made preparations. He is qualified by training and experience. He has applied himself on the job, and moved up from teller to head teller with its added responsibilities. *He has indicated to his superior he is interested in the new job.* His fiance is in accord with his wishes. Now let's use our Huna tools.

John, being skilled in formulating a prayer, takes time to see whether he and his low self are satisfied with the results after they have been attained. If the low self has a deep emotional attachment to his old place of work, or if it feels the new branch is too far away and balks at going to work through heavy traffic, a doubt may be raised. The manager at the Balboa Branch may be a person John does not like because of his attitude toward his subordinates, or he may have a reputation of questionable honesty. It may be even that John's low self does not wish to assume the new and added responsibilities that go with the job. If these factors are important to the low self, it may react with reluctance, fear and dislike.

If the low self projects confidence and eagerness to go along with the move, John will go ahead with his programming.

John will now write down his objective, stating in positive terms *what* he wants: a position as assistant manager of the Balboa Branch. (Since he undoubtedly knows the salary of this position, he need not name the sum; however, to be specific, he should add "for the prescribed salary" for his protection in that area.)

He must specify that his request will be for the good of all concerned, and must not hurt another in any way. If this request is granted and would deprive someone more deserving or better qualified, John must understand the Law cannot follow through in his favor.

A clear, unchanging mental picture of the desire is now made, *as if the condition had already been brought about.* John will see himself driving to the Balboa Branch office, greeting his new boss and meeting his new associates. He will sit down at his new desk and go through the motions of assuming his new responsibilities. He may visualize further going out with Mary later that evening to celebrate and talk of their coming marriage, even going out to look at condominiums. He will see himself complimented by his superior for a job well done. *He is on the way up the ladder.*

John will memorize his picture and rehearse it so nothing can change it. This mental picture is a thing which in Huna is believed to be made of the shadowy substance of the low self. All memories are believed to be made of the shadowy substance of the low self. All memories are believed to be microscopic bits of this substance molded in some way to embody the original thought or mental impression. But, as each memory is made up of a train of impressions the tiny and invisible thought-forms or impressions are tied together by threads of the shadowy substance. Modern psychology calls this "an association of ideas" in memory training.

If the job is indeed right for John and John right for the job, it will come to pass according to his programming. However, if some one in another branch has seniority, or some added qualification John does not possess (whether John feels this is "right" or not) and that other person is chosen assistant manager of the Balboa Branch, John must not react with negativity. This destructive thinking has set many people back in their progress. Know that everything happens for a positive reason. That reason may be nothing more than the blunt fact that the other fellow is more qualified. It may be this is a lesson in patience and perseverance for John, *or there may be something coming that is better for John as well as his employer.* Trust your high self. It can see further down the road than your limited middle self. Often a setback is a blessing in disguise.

How Long, Lord?

It is important to send the daily picture of the desired effect to the high self *without the slightest change* when the daily gift of *vital force* is submitted. As the prayer begins to be answered, *do give thanks at once.* Now the pattern is becoming crystalized, and continued prayer is needed to impress your low self to keep its faith strong. If the prayer is slow in being answered, a day of doubt and discouragement may upset the low self to the point of refusing to continue the daily repetition, and the entire prayer will be negated. *Pray without ceasing.*

Some things *take time.* Sometimes conditions behind the scenes, such as with social or business contacts and agreements, must follow a normal course of operation.

When prayer was submitted for the sale of one of my

books, several mediums (unknown to each other) told me, "The publisher who is interested in your work has not yet been organized." They were all right. Within a year after the business was formed, my books were brought to their attention and accepted very quickly. *But it took five years for that publisher to establish his business.*

When only small changes in the future are desired, the high self can often bring instant answers to prayer. When conditions must be restored to a former state, as in healing the body, the answer can be in the order of the miracle, but only if enough *vital force* is made available to the high self to make the immediate changes needed to remove a bad physical condition to normal harmony. Review the chapter on breathing.

Where a major change is needed at once, do pray constantly—and get others to pray with you. Many high selves involved in any request, be it helping or healing, increases the surcharge of *vital force* for one in need. Prayers offered daily with emotions aroused by the pressing need, plus hopeful faith in the answer, often speed the results in a most gratifying manner.

Thought-forms are likened to seeds by the Kahunas. These clusters make up the mental image of the condition prayed for. Picture the high self as one possessing a garden. It accepts the seeds which are floated along the shadowy cord on the flow of proffered *vital force*, and once accepted as worthy, these seeds are planted in the garden so they may grow into fruitful plants. Water your seeds daily! Offer them the sunshine of your positive thinking. *Don't dig them up to see if they're growing!* Some plants take longer to come to fruition than others. *Know the harvest will come because this is the Law.*

If *time* is a matter of prime importance, by all means put that into your programming. When asking for a sum of money to pay the rent or make a car payment, the due date of the note must be considered. A bank or finance company takes a dim view of late payments; penalties must be paid, regardless of the conditions or circumstances.

We *do* get what we pray for, so make sure this is what you want. A certain young lady programmed for a job offering fringe benefits and a pay scale her present employment did not offer. She set a time limit of 30 days. Promptly on the last day a job offer was made, promising everything she asked for. But no more. She learned very quickly the new surroundings were total negativity, the reason for the large turnover. Her next programming considered relations and conditions as well.

Is husband programming valid? Yes, but be advised it takes longer. When you are dealing with conditions that may involve other human beings (who may be doing *their* special programming), conflicts may arise. Other variables must be taken into account. Your dream man may be involved in his own confrontations, involving geography as well as physics. A certain person known to me was, on later calculations, actually on three occasions in the same vicinity at the same time as the man she eventually met and married. *The time was not ripe.* For everything there is a time and a season. *Know*—that eventually, time, space and conditions will come to a point of oneness.

Another caution on health. When you have a health challenge, *do not take yourself off the medication your doctor has given you to put your body chemically in balance.* Some people do this, in the fond hope the high self will automatically *make them well.* Please continue your medication *with* your meditation and programming. If, at some time the doctor decides as he checks your approved medical tests there is indeed a change and the medication may be changed or discontinued, so be it. Thank your high self for the healing given, but only when there is evidence this has been accomplished.

A man I know, a life-long diabetic, decided he had sufficient faith in his high self to heal himself. *This is not the decision of the middle self.* Only the high self can determine *when* and *if* such healing can take place. When I visited him at the hospital he wondered why he was not healed. The Kahunas had a good phrase for it: *when the patient is worthy.*

Can We Program Others? Yes, Cautiously!

Always, in programming, be it for self or others, the *key word* is the old Kahuna caution: *no hurt to others.* If what you desire is not for the good of *all* concerned, it is not valid. Every mother should take this caution to heart, which brings us to an important decision: children. May we program them? How? To what extent? Again, common sense is the answer, overshadowed by the Huna caution. Is it for *their* good? Yes, children may be programmed, but even they have free will. State specifically *who* you are and that you wish to help them to help themselves. Then add *how* and *why*, assuring them that this is for their highest good. If it is *not*, your high self will not carry it through, and certainly their high self will reject the coaching. The Kahunas went with the Law. So must you.

When the person is not mentally competent, he may still be sent the healing energy, even though it may be no more than a silent prayer. It will be heard.

A nurse in a psychiatric ward told of a woman, sullen and withdrawn for weeks, assigned to her care. Nancy sat quietly by the bedside and asked her low self to bring *vital force* to her own high self, asking that this healing energy be given to the patient. The woman looked up after some time and uttered the first words spoken in months. She knew *someone finally cared.* Her progress was slow but steady. *Somebody somewhere was listening.*

Huna-trained, Nancy was painfully aware that with many of the people committed here, the low self or the middle self *was not at home.* Whether this condition was emotional, drug or alcohol induced, did not matter. Sometimes it was obvious to note other entities were in possession of the body. There was no control. Like the Kahunas of old, the medical teams had to work with the remaining self, hoping the other would return to assume its normal function. An awareness of Huna would greatly help people involved in such situations. Psychiatrists who have studied the Huna philosophy report great strides in their profession. The *light* will yet touch the darkest minds and make them whole.

The Kahunas taught man is a complete being only when the three selves are attuned, each performing its prescribed duty. The high self is part of the three-self man, and as such is *loved*, rather than worshipped.

The word used by the Kahunas for *worship* is *hoomana*, literally meaning "to create *vital force*."

This is the prayer secret. When we understand it, we know what is done with the *extra vital force* created. It is sent as a gift of love to the high self.

Vital force, then, is the *Life Force. With* it, we may ask for anything our heart desires. Without it, there can be no eternity.

Chapter XV
Living
The Huna
Principles

The externals of the reconstructed Huna system are admittedly cold. However, there is within them all the possibilities of the deep, warm response to the high self, and through it with ultimate God.

The concept of salvation is not a part of the Huna teachings. It was believed mankind could, however, be greatly helped knowing there was a high self, and that one could communicate with these beings, assured of guidance and protection under free will.

According to their mythology, the Huna system presents a theory of evolution in which units of consciousness evolve upward gradually from the group units of rocks and waters, through the vegetable kingdom to insects, birds and animals.

It was believed that in the course of evolution the animal called man became ready, and then a "god" came down and assumed the place of a middle self, living inside the animal body, training the low self, and causing changes in the brain to enable inductive reason to be used, also the "will." The animal mate of the first human was soon put into a deep sleep and the high self divided into male and female parts, the female part entering the female body. Could this be the origin of the Adam and Eve story of Genesis?

It is interesting to note that when it was divided into two parts to rule over two animals of opposite sexes, it lost its god-like powers. It could no longer see the future without help from above, nor could it change matter or directly control nature. Perhaps this is the original idea of a god incarnating in a man animal, and so making the supreme sacrifice of itself, to make possible the salvation or continuing upward evolution, of living things on earth. The separated selves were not reunited until their evolvement was complete and they graduated to the high self status again, finishing the cycle.

The three selves of man must work out their evolvement in unison and graduation occurs only when all have evolved sufficiently to move to the next higher level. Each self is associated with the next self above it in the triune man. Thus the middle self trains the low self so it eventually may become a middle self of a savage, and when its functions have been fulfilled, is born into a savage body. It is now a middle self, ready to begin earning, through several lives, the use of inductive reason. Into this new savage body comes a new low self which has just graduated up from the animal kingdom. It begins its schooling under the new middle self. With and above them is a new high self, who supervises the human low and middle self in their evolvement.

The high self reaches out to the lesser two, probably in its shadowy body, in dreams and meditation. We need only to call out and help will be given. It is not for us to understand the function of the high self, only to know it is there, operating with the Law.

An apt illustration is the relationship of a man and his pet. The animal is cared for by man, but for the most part, it does what it pleases. If it gets into trouble, it runs to its master for help and protection. The man understands the animal, and it, according to its limited nature, understands the man. But the animal does not always understand the why and wherefore of its master. Often the master's activities and his purposes remain a confusing mystery to the pet. So it is with us. Our finite minds cannot grasp the infinite.

God is unknowable to Mankind. We understand only the divine attributes, and these often with difficulty:

God is omnipotent, meaning all powerful. God is omnipresent, meaning present in all places at the same time. God is omniscient, meaning He has infinite knowledge. Certainly God is knowledgeable of mankind at all times.

In Huna we cannot pray directly to the high self, nor to the company of high selves. All must go through the proper channel: low self, at the direction of the middle self sets the telepathic communication in operation. The high self, consequently, reaches out to the high selves beyond.

Likewise are Christians urged to address all prayers to God directly through Christ. Jesus offered to pray to the Father for the disciples, and in this respect He stood as the Christ or the high self.

The teachings of Jesus, traced to the Enochian doctrines on human behavior, have much in common with Huna. As the Christ, Jesus is considered universal in nature. He demonstrated the ability to contact the Father at will. Explaining his miracles, he pointed out it was *through* the Father those things were made possible. The Father worked *through* him and seemed to be *in* him. The Huna sensation experienced when contact with the high self is made through the mechanism of the connecting thread of the shadowy body material gives one the feeling the high self is indeed *inside* one.

In healing work, Jesus at times used a physical stimulus to accompany his command, indicating strong powers of suggestion. An example is the blind man whose eyes were healed when Jesus covered them with mud and spittle. This is similar to the Kahuna use of a physical stimulus to accompany and strengthen suggestion. The Kahunas also ordered their patients to make amends for hurts done to others, then used some physical stimuli to aid suggestion in draining off guilt fixations. This enabled the low self of the patient to be restored to a condition in which it could be healed by the high self. This condition was one in which the "path" of contact with the high self was to be unblocked. It was the condition necessary to the restoration of faith, without which no healing was thought possible.

Instant healing, according to Huna, was possible only through the high self. This term, more than any other, has puzzled students of Huna trained in a western culture that considers such experience under the label of "magic" or superstition. But Huna is in essence, simple and relatively uncomplicated.

Instant healing is obtained by deciding that we want a future in which we are not ill, but healed. When we ask our high self to heal a broken bone instantly, and it is done, we can say that the high self changed the future *instantly* for us, so far as the broken bone is concerned. Here we are free agents and must decide what we want and to *hold* that decision as the initial step in getting help from the high self. This healing help applies to the healing of our bank account as well as to the healing of other circumstances.

The future, according to Huna, is chiefly constructed by the high self, and it lays out the main points in the life of the individual for which it is responsible. But the day-to-day future is built by taking the thoughts, hopes, fears and plans of the two lower selves and using them as figurative "seeds" from which to grow the events of subsequent tomorrows. *Free will* is the inalienable right of the two lesser selves in furnishing the materials to make future conditions and life events.

Dreams are the communications life-line of the high self. An aware middle self can use his dreams in a positive manner, solving his daily challenges, programming his future activities and when necessary, obtaining information not otherwise available.

Researching the background material for my Biblical novel, I needed more details on the illness of the King of Babylon. The Book of Daniel mentioned only: "...he was driven from among men, and did eat grass like an ox, and his body was wet with the dew of the heaven till his hair grew like eagles' feathers and nails like bird claws.''

Not much satisfaction, here. Theologians mouthed pious platitudes, but nothing of a practical nature. I directed my low self to ask the high self for an explanation as I was in the meditative state. The answer was a shocker: drugs.

But *what* drugs? The answer was prompt. Under the system, the King of Babylon was theoretically also High Priest, and as such he had access to the priestly drugs. His troubles multiplied when he took several of these together. I was given not only the origin of the drugs, but where these were obtained. But where to find further information on these ancient mixtures?

Now the high self changed the tactics. Onto my mental screen was flashed the image of a camel. Since I know only one camel, identification was easy. I called my former Huna student and explained what had happened, ending with the casual "What do you know about ancient drugs?"

Her startled silence was followed by an incredulous "No *way* could you possibly have known...that my subject for the thesis for my doctorate was...ancient drugs."

Huna *works*. All we need to do is to train the low self with loving firmness, expecting results. Tools will only work when you put them to work for you.

What about situations that appear to be linked to other lifetimes, such as conflicts with certain individuals, or even phobias? Can the low self tap the memory bank and obtain data that would help resolve such experiences rather than to obtain the services of a hypnotist?

Certainly, but this is a slower method, though to my thinking, more valid, since it comes from within *you* and is brought out under *your* control. Caution is suggested here, for this is not a plaything and must be used with the utmost discretion. Stored memories are not open for curious scrutiny for scrutiny's sake. When there is, however, an honest request for a legitimate purpose, the high self will bring forth the information desired in a manner the middle self can understand and utilize.

For years I was puzzled over my fear of water, for I was fascinated by it, so long as my feet touched solid ground. When my thirteen-year old Girl Scouts applied for their swimming badge, the instructor, knowing of my inability to swim, casually suggested I join the ranks. I accepted the challenge, even to attending twice a week evening practice sessions at the pool.

One night I mastered the art of floating, and suddenly the old feeling of panic was gone in deep water. All I had to do was to turn over and relax! I felt as though a weight of water had been lifted from my chest.

That night as I drifted off to sleep I wondered vaguely why I had not learned this valuable lesson before. My mind went back over many opportunities missed in past summers when my children were small. Even in my younger days, I was the nonswimming beauty poolside; the only dry one among the children growing up by the Neckar River. From earliest childhood I was *afraid* of water, haunted by the fear of drowning.

There was an interesting dream, that night, so real and vivid I *knew* it had really happened, though oddly, I was a young boy and the sea setting completely foreign to me. I was with a group of men evacuating a sinking boat. We were crowded into small lifeboats as the sea mountained white foamed waves around us. Interestingly, I was actually *two* people: the boy in the boat, shivering and cold, and myself, standing off to the side observing the scene. Suddenly a huge wave washed over the fragile craft, and I could feel the sheer terror of it breaking over me as the sea pulled it into the deep, and I woke up, wet and cold.

What actually happened? Inadvertently, I had regressed myself, going *backwards* while in a meditative state. The pool experience nudged the memory of that past experience and brought it into my conscious mind. The

116

low self accepted the unconscious order and brought the fear to the surface. I knew then I must learn how to swim and cancel the fear completely.

Passing the swimming test with flying colors, even the required dive from the board, I knew the crucial test was now to take myself to the open sea. It was not an easy thing to do, but within a few weeks I felt at home in the deep, secure in the feeling that if tired, I need only turn over and float with the tide.

On occasion I have used the regression method to find out why there is often a personal challenge between myself and certain people. Not surprisingly, the fault is usually with me, for attitude is an important factor in matters pertaining to self improvement. We all have the same challenges, and these need not be detailed here other than to identify them as lessons in patience, tolerance, humility and compassion. When I express eagerness to work on these for *self* improvement, I am clearly shown where and how in the past I had gone astray. In almost every case, involvement concerned something left unfinished. The dreams coming forth were not always clear dreams or nice dreams or even understanding dreams, but my dolphin got the messages and brought them bravely forth. A more aware middle self cooperated in most cases, and we are, hopefully, putting our house in order.

There are probably many ways to regress yourself, but the most safe and practical is to use suggestology on the low self while in a light state of meditation, preferably just before drifting off to sleep. Review all that has happened that day, by recalling your experiences in reverse. Then pass lightly over the week, the month and year. Years wing backwards very quickly, the highlights of your childhood as far back as memory goes. Let yourself drift to sleep, holding firmly to the challenge on which you are presently working. Record your dream promptly on waking, noting especially the emotions felt, the color and intensity of the surroundings and the clothing worn.

Double entry dreams, where you appear to be watching the action as well as participating in it are usually past life experiences. You may or may not be aware that your acting self is not in a familiar physical body. But there will be an inate *knowing* that the person observed is *you.*

Seldom do regressed experiences come out in one dream alone unless one particular experience will bring you to an intuitive realization. One such experience concerned the death of my children when I was in a black body. The agony felt by the mother was so intense at the murder I woke with tears choking me and had to go back at once to change the situation. Not that this action changed the experience once lived, but it did neutralize the emotions which where carried over into a subsequent lifetime.

Suggestology is a tedious undertaking, yes, sometimes taking months or years. But it is *safe* because this method is under the control of your middle self and the protection of the high self. I have been working on one dream experience going back to Babylonian days for more than ten years. Someday it will all come together.

Let me remind you, this is not to find out what a fascinating character you were in the past. Forget your "historical" identity! Identification of such can be a shock. The important thing is to receive your past imperfections and to review past unlearned lessons. The low self, having no reasoning power, will bring you anything requested. Do ask the high self for protection and guidance and work within the triunity principles for safe, sensible results to put your house in order.

Chapter XVI
The
Mystery
Teachings

The traditional mythology of the ancient Hawaiians, containing the esoteric code of the Kahunas, concerns the working of the cosmic forces and detail legends of the submerged continent of Lemuria — Mu — once a flourishing civilization in the area now the Pacific Ocean. According to their legends, the present islands are the mountain tops of that inundated territory, its history retained only in their poetic folklore.

Included in Leinani Melville's translation *Children of the Rainbow* are legends and myths concerning the people of Mu, including sacred chants and temple prayers, many of which contain concepts akin to the religions and folklore of other ancient cultures. Many of these traditions had a deep spiritual meaning, which unfortunately became lost with the Christianizing of the islands.

The Polynesians believed that all that has been created was as a result of the marriage of gods. The first four gods were the four great primary forces, a name given them during earth's first great civilization: "In the beginning there was no light, life or sound in the world. A boundless night called Po enveloped everything, over which Tanaoa (darkness) and Mutu-hei (silence) reigned supreme. Then the god of light separated from Tanaoa, fought him, drove him away and confined him to the night. Then the god Ono (sound) was evolved from Atea (light) and banished silence. From all this struggle was Atauana (dawn) born. Atea married Atauana and they created earth, animals and man."

In his intriguing series on Mu, Col. James Church-ward details the similarities of the ancient Coptic (Egyptian) religious practices to the Huna beliefs of the Polynesians. The Egyptians also believed all was created as a result of the marriage of the gods, or cosmic forces, and that Mu was the motherland of Mankind. In his series on Mu, Churchward details research verified by inscriptions and recorded records. When Lemuria was submerged, breaking off from the Asian mainland, many of the inhabitants apparently migrated to Atlantis via the American continent, taking the ancient teachings with them.

The triunity of man appears in many American Indian cultures on both continents. The teachings crop up in prayers and chants in words long forgotten and meanings reduced to superstitions.

The Cherokee Indians, native to the southeast and Appalachia, to this day still recite an ancient "love charm" hauntingly reminiscent of the Kahuna interpretation of the action of the shadowy "finger" projected by the shadowy body of low self. Read again the symbol of the spider's web with flies caught in it on page 80 and compare it to the Cherokee charm:

> "Now our souls have met, never to part. O
> Black Spider, you have brought down your
> web! Her soul you have wrapped up in your
> web! You may hold her soul in your web so
> that it shall never get through the meshes."

Other researchers believe there is a definite relationship between the "old ways" of the Polynesians to ancient practices in other cultures. Baird T. Spalding, in his *Life and Teachings of the Masters of the Far East* cites some interesting parallels, detailing as well the ability the old Hawaiians to call the fish to shore and to "talk sharks out of areas where they were not welcome.

It remained for Max Freedom Long to touch on the Holy of Holies in his investigation into the ancient teachings. In his book *The Huna Code In Religions*, he challenges theologians with the flat declaration that Huna was known to the high priesthood of many of the only civilizations predating antiquity. He raised some interesting questions in his earlier books, then confounded everyone by answering them in fact.

Religious belief of earlier training given most adults frequently causes fixations, he asserts, especially where people are told to interpret the Bible literally and without question, as in certain fundamentalist denominations.

The readings of the ancient lore as found in the Bible are of great value in helping the middle self come to an understanding of what was real and genuine, and what is added dogma. There is much Huna in the Bible. The rule to follow was that only the actual words of Jesus were to be trusted in the New Testament. But after his death a mass of dogmatic theology was invented and added, as were rites and doctrines which, like the misconceptions surrounding the earlier ideas of blood sacrifice, were evidently inaugurated to impress the people and to make the teachings work better.

He has a case in point. All through the New Testament are references to the "mystery teachings" of Jesus, but these were never defined in scriptures. We are told Jesus instructed his disciples in secret, talking only in parables to the masses. In other words, these were the outer teachings (exoteric) spoken in general by the uninitiated; the inner teachings (esoteric) were given only to, and understood by, the initiates. Huna, meaning "secret" to all appearances, is the mystery teachings of the ancients' Holy of Holies—the Bible—in his investigation into the ancient teachings.

Why there was a cult of secrecy is not made clear.

There are, obviously, passages in the Old Testament that could have been written only by initiates into the secret lore, showing through their use of symbols and code keys, common to Huna, that there are several forms of "sin" which may cause the blocking of shadowy cord to the high self—God.

Again and again we are told these blockings can and will be removed when the proper tools are applied, but what they were, and how this would be done was never explained.

The New Testament gives evidence Jesus affected sweeping reforms to break down the archaic practices, hardly understood, to which the Jews clung for so long. His aim was to make known how these stumbling blocks may be removed, that man might reach his high self at will.

The Four Gospels all contain knowledge of Huna. The disciples were initiated into the Huna lore, instructed by use of the "sacred" language of the Kahunas. Because of this knowledge of the sacred language, they set about preserving in writing the directions for removing fixations and becoming freed from the clutches of spirits stealing the *vital force* from the man.

To the student interested in Long's revelation and practical arguments on this matter, I would suggest a thorough reading of his *The Secret Science At Work*. Clearly the scope of such investigation would be a book by itself. Long's recovery of the ancient "way of life" also referred to as "the true light" in Egypt is worth investigating. It could well be the spiritual answer to Mankind's search for his soul.

From all the studies made of the words spoken by Jesus, one thing emerges with startling clarity. Jesus taught a way of bringing about a normal relationship between the three selves. Such normal relationship is the sum total of "salvation." He did not teach that he, personally, was a direct means of salvation and that one might be forgiven his sins and be made physically, mentally or morally, by the simple act of believing that he, Jesus, was able to bring about such salvation.

Man must bring about his own salvation. Jesus offered the instructions, the methods to be used, and to those near him, he offered help in putting those methods to use. He instructed his disciples to offer the same help to those who could not use the methods themselves—particularly those who were unable to free themselves of fixations or spirit influences, so they could open their paths to their own high selves.

Jesus came to teach men how to work out their own salvation, not to offer it as a mystic gift. Jesus distinguished the Lord (high self) from Jehovah by calling him Father. He was not ultimate God. He was the Haku of the Kahunas, The Lord of the divided waters" or of the vital force which must be shared or divided between the lower selves and the high self if the latter is to play its vital part in the life of Mankind.

Long's purpose of separating the teachings of Jesus from dogma was to use the test of Huna. This colossal undertaking is best exemplified in the following pages.

Jesus began his ministry by reading a passage from Isaiah. The prophet was a great Huna initiate, as translation into the sacred language reveals without doubt. The incident is recorded in Luke (4:16–21):

"And he came to Nazareth where he had been brought up; and he entered, as was his custom into the synagogue on the sabbath day, and stood up to read.

"And there was delivered unto him the book of the prophet Isaiah. And he opened the book, and found the place where it was written, 'The Spirit of the Lord is upon me, Because he anointed me to preach the good tidings to the poor; He hath sent me to proclaim release to the captives, And recovering of sight to the blind, To set at Liberty them that are bruised, To proclaim the acceptable year of the Lord.' And he closed the book and gave it back to the attendants and sat down; and the eyes of all in the synagogue were fastened on him. And he began to say unto them, 'Today hath this scripture been fulfilled in your ears.' ''

Jesus accepted the prediction that a new and greater prophet of the Huna order would arise, and he knew that in himself he embodied the fulfillment of the prophecies. In the prophecies he was described as the Son of God, and as one united to God (the high self Father or Aumakua of Huna). Realizing his own union with his high self, and being able to heal because of that union, he began at the start of his ministry to teach men that such a union was possible and that he had accomplished it.

At no time did he claim *that no other person could attain a similar union.* On the contrary, he urged constantly others should do likewise. When they were about to stone him for saying "I and the Father are one." Jesus answered the acccusers "Is it not written in your law, I said, Ye are gods?" Referring further to the Psalms, he disarmed them further with his final argument. "If he called them gods, unto whom the word of God came, and the scripture cannot be broken, say ye of him whom the Father hath sanctified and sent into the world, thou blasphemeth because I said I am the son of God?"

In the places in his teachings in which Jesus spoke as if he were God or the Father, and not a man, he was following the ancient Huna custom. He taught simply that it was impossible for a man in the flesh to unite with his own high self, whom he called "The Father" (that dwelleth in me) and to become *one* in this union.

The high self is given the title of the Holy Spirit as it descends on Jesus as a dove during the baptism by John at the River Jordan. Each self of man is a spirit to the Kahuna, the Aumakua being "the holy one."

John, in writing of the Last Supper, gives the valuable last instruction of Jesus to his disciples at that time.

"A new commandment I give unto you, *that ye love one another.*"

Nothing could have summed up the new covenant than that commandment. It is the most revealing of his Huna teachings.

In the symbolic presentation of the communion rite, he shed no blood at all. The entire rite embodied a restatement of the great basic principles of Huna, the knowledge of which makes each man and woman able not only to obtain cleansing for "sin," but to make contact with the high self—which is to "become one with the Father."

This was the goal of Jesus' teachings.

Chapter XVII
Self-Awareness through Huna

There has been much concern among modern students of Huna over the loss of the ancient Huna prayer chants. True, the "outer" rituals have been recovered and duly recorded, but what other private ceremonia was chanted silently by the Kahunas when they evoked their sacred magic? How can the system be effectively practiced without the forgotten prayer methods?

The prayer chants, as such, were probably utilized to put the ancient Kahunas into altered states of consciousness. From antiquity various aids were popular, from the primitive cultures to so-called "higher" civilizations. The American Indians observed the movement of the waters or the flame of an open fire. The Druids contemplated the trees and flowers and studied cloud formations. The Babylonians studied sheep entrails and the effect of certain oils on water. The priestesses of the Temple Oracles inhaled aromatic vapors for trans-readings and the priests helped themselves to mind-altering drugs to demonstrate their powers.

Let me say it again: Huna *is simple,* Huna *is practical and* Huna *is adaptable.* The teachings were valid among the primitives of Polynesia and worked equally well for the alchemists of the ziggurats, and the secret societies of the pyramids, though there is a span of eight thousand years or more between the cultures. Surely this adaptability will adjust itself equally to encompass our computer age.

The Age of Aquarius—the mind age—is already upon us. People are speaking as glibly of their alpha-experiences and brain-wave frequencies as they once touted the cost of their analyst and worth of their broker. Bio-feedback machines are replacing the sacraments—we have come full circle and can use the ancient tool, Huna, *simply by using our minds.*

The soul must be recognized, understood and fed. One cannot move on the Huna path without becoming spiritual. Religion touches only on creeds and orthodoxy and dogma. Perhaps this is why Huna was considered secret for so long. Spirituality is attained only by the individual working on his own evolvement *upward.* No one can do it for you.

Since its recovery by Long, many people have studied and applied the Huna principles over a period of years. Using no more than the basic outline, they agree the principle works when the tools are used properly. True, no one walks on water or over fire—yet—but all admit the practical application has brought them a peace of mind not enjoyed by alternate religious psychology. It fits very comfortably into the modern life style, for without realizing it, western man has reached out hungrily to the eastern cults and adapted them to his own life style. Their methods vary.

The popular meditation classes often use music to go to altered states of consciousness. Besides "soothing the savage beast" music creates moods, depending on the purpose in mind. The military has used martial music since the beginning of time to stir the people to patriotic fervor, or to rouse the flagging spirits of battle-weary troops. Lovers have their favorite tunes. Business has learned the psychology of music, frequently piping it into hospitals, banks and even department stores to create a certain frame of mind. Mood music? Why not?

For years I used Beethoven's music in my writing studio without realizing the composer wrote from that level himself. Tchaikovsky is another mood-spinner, especially for sentimental settings, as is Brahms and Debussy. The "1812 Overture" on the other hand, has set the stage for every battle-scene from the Bablylonian assault on Tyre to the storming of Iwo Jima by American marines. The mood sets the stage, and our thoughts perform accordingly with the use of our imaginations.

Thoughts are the key to Huna. Thoughts sent out return according to their conception. They bring back what was sent out, nothing more, nothing leas.

Know Yourself. Understand why you are as you are. Study your low self's physiology, its habits, instincts and peculiarities as well as its pattern of behavior. Study especially the food likes and dislikes of your middle self. What your animal likes or dislikes may be the reason for your own food preferences. It may, likewise, be the answer to food allergies.

Let's consider food in the light of Huna. Herbivorous low selves prefer salads, greens and raw vegetables to a marked degree. Carnivorous animals on the other hand, feel deprived without their daily ration of meat (often requested three times daily) to the exclusion of a balanced nutritious program.

Mothers whose low self is herbivorous, raising children with carnivorous low selves, will find out quickly enough they cannot impose their dietary preferences upon their offspring. Likewise mothers with a carnivorous low self must be aware their herbivorous oriented offspring must be catered to with diets that may not suit her theories on nutrition. In this field, a knowledge of Huna would aid parents in the care and feeding of their offspring. It would certainly have saved me concern when my own brood was growing up, explaining at the same time some interesting food peculiarities among them and their friends. The deer and rabbits did best on vegetables; the seal and bear loved meat and fish with equal passion, as did the lazy lion cub. The domestic cats could not get through the day without a quart or more of milk; my dolphin abhorred it. The goat ate *anything*, and the chimpanzee's passion for bananas never failed to amaze us. *You are what you eat* is certainly not an idle phrase. *You like what your low self likes to eat* is equally important.

The low self, when understood according to its inherent animal make-up, is more easily loved and trained. I know few people who are not proud of their low self. Those who are ashamed of it have an understandable problem, usually manifested in crippling arthritis. A change of attitude is highly recommended.

Study not only your low self but the low selves of those about you, particularly your fellow employees.

A young lady working in a personnel office learned to "read" those working with her, treating them according to the low self her practical training has taught her they are. She is considered an astute judge of character with a rare gift of communication with others. All she did was to apply Huna to her daily work!

"Before studying Huna I simply *reacted* to people, seldom understanding *why*," she confessed. "Now I'm at peace with myself. Huna has taught me how to cope with others and *to put myself into perspective*. My middle self and my low self are partners."

As partners, we must of course function according to the prescribed role. But even partners have misunderstanding at times. Be very careful not to automatically blame the low self for *everything* that may go wrong. *It may be the fault of the middle self!*

Another minister and I were asked to participate in a church service in another area. Afterwards the pastor offered each of us an envelope as a donation for our services. My thanks were as prompt as the refusal to accept the money: I suggested the money be put into the church's building fund. The other speaker agreed, without hesitation. Not until later did it occur to me my decision should have been made privately, for it put the other speaker on the spot, and she had no choice but to follow through with my decision.

My first impulse was to chew on my dolphin's tail, and a royal raking it was! *How could you do such a stupid thing?!* He told me loud and clear: *but you told me to!*

Then it hit me. My low self was doing *exactly* what he was ordered to do, nothing more, nothing less. If the action was wrong, then it was the fault of the director, the middle self, who should have rationalized the impulsive gesture and made whatever acknowledgement in private. Another thought hit me. I did not need the money, but probably the other speaker did....

I spent the next fifteen minutes apologizing to the dolphin, telling him what he did was out of love, and that I, as the middle self, had neglected to do my job. The middle self was the stupid one, not my low self!

Treat your low self as an intelligent being, a partner in the learning lessons of life. Assume the blame when you are at fault, and your low self will not feel put down. Since the middle self was at fault, the middle self called the pastor in the morning and apologized, asking that the other speaker be contacted privately and the money given. Apologies were also made to the speaker for my presumptuousness. Surprisingly she laughed, saying she always donated whatever gift was offered for these engagements. All that worry for nothing? Not really. A valuable lesson was learned. Now, before blaming the low self for an action, I take a careful inventory to see where the fault *really* lies. The middle self, too, must learn her lessons.

Self realization comes only when we understand the function of *each* self, and live accordingly. This is why the application of the Huna tools are so important and a thorough understanding of their function cannot be overemphasized. *Thoughts* are the key to the Huna secret, their construction and direction of vital importance. Thoughts sent out return according to their conception. They can bring back only what was sent out. A pure consciousness experiences all within itself, reflecting only that which it is in reality. Life is a polarity of opposites: love and hate, purity and impurity, health and sickness. A loving heart can only visualize loving conditions. A kind mind thinks only kindness. A pure consciousness reflects only purity. In other words, the basis of giving kindness is receiving kindness. The basis of understanding spiritual nature is to be a spiritual nature. Like begets like. We are a reflection of ourselves.

Jesus said: "I come not to change the Laws but to uphold them." Few understood him. He instructed his followers to observe two vital commandments. The first: *"Love the Lord your God with all your heart and with all your might and with all your mind."* The second commandment cautioned them: *"Love your neighbor as yourself."*

Translated into Huna, what do these commandments mean? *To be aware of your high self and to love your high self completely.* In Huna, the high self is not worshipped, but *loved.*

To love the Lord your God means to love the spirit of truth within. When mankind finally understands that the total source of supply is within, he will know he can draw from the limitless infinite substance and he will not *need to seek outside for fulfillment of what is within.* He will not seek to know what the Law is, and how to use the Law: he will *be* the Law, and it will work *for* him, *as* him. *It is done according to your belief.* This is self-realization.

To love your neighbor (meaning of course your fellow human being) means to have compassion on him and to help him in every way possible. To love your neighbor may be no more than to send him kindly thoughts of love and peace of mind, in his daily struggle with life. Again, it could mean to send him *vital force* energy when extra strength is needed, either as a help-aid or as a health-aid. This may be done simply by telling your low self to request your high self reach out to the high self of the person in need. Such a spiritual transfusion can lift another to the level where his lagging spirits are boosted, and thereafter he can help himself. *Love your neighbor as yourself*. By helping another you are helping yourself as well. This, too, is self-realization.

Once suggestion may be to form a circle similar to those held in a seance, but without calling on the spirits of the dead for help. The circle can be used as a source of *vital force*, each sitter donating a little, and the leader of the group creating the thought-forms of the "prayer" contacting the high self for assistance in this project.

The Kahunas made use of this *vital force* in several ways. The *vital force* is increased in the body by a simple act of will. The low self soon learns the trick and the presence of the extra charge creates a tingle in the hands or any part of the body. Care must be taken in the choice of sitters, for such a circle. Each member must be in normal health and of good mental balance. Such work may lead to psychic experiences, where the spirits of the dead (or the low self spirits) are seen or felt. Great caution should therefore be taken and the help of an experienced medium is requested for supervision. Obsession is possible.

Deep breathing with a willed effort to accumulate an extra charge of low *vital force* is an excellent stimulus as a starter. The leader then recites an affirmation, directing the combined energy be sent to an individual while everyone concentrates on his name, or his face, if this is known. When possible, notify the person being helped by telling him the time and date the energy circle is being formed. Ask that he go off by himself and go into the silence. He *will* feel the energy and be uplifted by the experience, as many so helped have attested.

Our own small circle began in a modest way with only seven members. When Sue missed a meeting because of a light respiratory infection, her husband Ron "stood in" as proxy for her in the center of the circle. We projected love and energy and healing for about sixty seconds. Later she shared with us she fell into a deep sleep about the same hour, and did not waken until morning, refreshed and feeling her old self.

The low self is very susceptible to this type of communication. Where much *vital force* is needed, such as a person gravely ill or hospitalized as a result of accident, our small circle worked in absentia, projecting love and energy *daily*, each member sending *vital force* during their meditation period.

Remember in Huna, *all things are triune.* There is always a conscious being using a force or power to work with some form of matter, be it dense or etheric. The *vital force* is the energy used by the high self. The triune man has three voltages of the energy or electro-vital force. Huna recognizes three levels, grades or voltages of the energy, a voltage of each of the three selves. The *vital force* of the low self is of a certain voltage. It is stepped up for the middle self, and stepped up even higher for the high self. This type of energy is that used in instant healing, when the material substances in a bone-break are dissolved to etheric form and then re-solidified as an unbroken bone. This type of energy dissolves diseased tissue to etheric form and then re-solidifies it as new, healthy tissue. This type of energy is that used to regulate cold or heat in fire-walking.

Instant healing is sometimes considered with the righteous skepticism even by the serious Huna student. Our conscious mind often balks at something it cannot rationalize. But just because we cannot understand it does not mean it is not possible! It is always interesting to observe students involved in such a healing and to view their amazement when the "impossible" happens. One such was a member of our group, going through the teachings with considerable doubts because of her own medical background. Among her colleagues, the unexplainable was labeled "a miracle" and dismissed.

She called me one evening and announced most matter-of-factly "I'm to be hospitalized tomorrow for an undisclosed stomach disorder that will probably result in exploratory surgery. Please have the group send me energy. I'll send feedback via Chuck."

The next day Chuck called with the news that Rita

was also suffering a respiratory infection, but that testing was in progress. Later, the laboratory tests were conclusive. Cancer in the abdominal area. Surgery was slated as soon as the infection had cleared up.

Meanwhile the group went to work, each member sending Rita daily doses of *vital force* with the dedication so typical of Huna students. Later Rita shared with us she could *feel* that energy as she lay in her hospital bed. Feel it? It was as though she was plugged into a vibrating machine! Since each of us meditated at a different time of the day or night (many three times daily) this transference of *vital force* was projected almost around the clock. If any of us woke up at night, we sent a quick energy thought in Rita's direction, mentally *seeing her whole and going about her daily work.*

When the time for surgery came, another series of tests was made by the same technicians in the same laboratory. The doctors stared at each other in amazement. *No cancerous growth was in evidence.* A hurried conference was held. They told Rita at least they thought exploratory surgery should be undertaken as a precautionary measure. She shrugged and assured them they would find nothing. She knew what she had experienced, but how could she make them understand? The operation was performed: nothing was found. Rita waved their apologies aside. "That's all right, boys. I know exactly *why* you found nothing: *there was nothing there.*"

She was right. Whatever *had been* present was dissolved, and new tissue resolidified to healthy tissue. It could only be understood through Huna, by those knowing of the Huna method of calling on the combined high selves of the attendants of the healing circle. Let science play around with that concept for a while!

She confided to me later "I knew *exactly* what brought on this diseased conditon, and how my change of attitude and mind could change it, thanks to the Huna teachings. The infection has given me a "grace" period. I'll use it to heal myself." And she did.

Another case of instant healing is given here which was, though not observed by me personally, unique only in the faith of the people involved.

A baker of a large food chain told me of a Filipino butcher who cut off his thumb while cutting up a side of beef. Immediately he picked it up from the floor and stuck it back in place as his fellow Filipinos encircled him in a silent prayer offering. After a brief interval the butcher asked for a bandage to wrap his hand. His dumb-founded supervisor wanted to rush him to the hospital, but the butcher shrugged and bandaged his hand, then proceeded to return to work. The next morning he came in, his hand free. The injured thumb? He held up his hand. *The thumb was intact, clean, and apparently healed.* The only ones who did not question the happening were his Filipino coworkers. They understood the Huna principle. None attempted to explain it. The Islanders had long given up teaching western man their ancient secrets.

Jesus, the Nazarene Kahuna put it succinctly: *Thy faith has made thee whole.*

Max Long founded a new church, the Huna Fellowship, in 1945, to be incorporated as a non-profit organization under the laws of the State of California. Membership in the Huna Fellowship was open to all applicants of sound mind and morals, regardless of religious or racial affiliations. Experimental members would give what time and talent they had to experimentation. Sustaining members would offer their various contributions and help and encourage the experimenters. Associate members would do what they could, watch progress sympathetically and spread the news of the rediscovery of the Huna system. All members would be eligible for such benefits as may be made available when and if healers could be developed.

In due time it was anticipated that a foundation would be established for or within the organization and places be provided for church use and hospitalization. It was a Utopian idea.

In practice, physicians of the several schools, psychologists and healers would work together. Much of the healing done by the Kahunas was the slow or psychological kind. This form of healing may yet turn out to be a great help to medical, surgical and manipulative healing.

It was suggested that patients applying for healing would present medical records, then be conditioned by psychologists to get them free from guilt and other hindering complexes. This would save time of those who would then contact the high self and construct the prayer for instant (or less than instant) healing. There must be no retrogression. All available knowledge must be used wherever possible.

Perhaps there should even be a definite innovation in the healing of social tangles and circumstantial ills. Healing in this classification would begin directly with the use of psychological conditioning after a preliminary study of the individual case. A decision would be reached by a joint effort of the patient and the psychologist to determine what changes in conditions were to be made. After that, the healer would take over to complete the work of presenting the prayer for a changed "future" to the high self.

Work under such a system would be of far more importance than would appear at first glance. It would have many ramifications, its implications vital to health and happiness of all concerned.

There is no reason such a program could not be adapted to our western culture. The psycho-religious system of Huna was known to have worked right up to modern times, in the capable hands of the Kahuna healers. It is simple, practical and devoid of dogma and superstition. It can be understood by scientists as well as religionists without offending either.

We have also the scientific knowledge which may help to bring the ancient basic system to further perfection and workability. Having inherited mathematics and astronomy from the elder races, we have been able to bring both to much higher stages of development. Huna, with its broad, all-encompassing concepts, could give humanity the spiritual transfusion it needs for survival.

Surely, if there are sufficient numbers who can see the shining possibilities, and who will set to work with a will, spreading the information about Huna—and not incidentally applying the tools to their own living, thus setting an example to others—there could result, in a short time, an organization of such size and scope that undertakings would quickly become an accomplished fact.

Hopefully, then, the firebrand tossed into the heavens by Max Freedom Long will be taken up by far-sighted enthusiasts, and Huna, THE SECRET, will unfold to become the salvation for the future, just as it was the hope and inspiration of the past.

About the Author:

Noted teacher and author, Erika Nau holds a doctorate degree in metaphysical philosophy, and a teaching certificate from Huna Research Associates in Cape Girardeau, Missouri. Dr. Nau has been writing successfully in many fields since her youth, but favors metaphysics and historical fiction. She is the author of *The Huna Handbook*, a text used in her courses; and *Angel in the Rigging*, a fiction work about early America, published by Berkley-Putnam. As a member of the Marine Corps she was transferred to San Diego in 1944 while a reporter for *The Chevron*, being the first woman editor on the staff. She and her husband have resided there since and are the parents of five grown children.

Annotated Bibliography

Huna Research Associates

Max Freedom Long established Huna Research Associates in 1945 to assist him in putting the Huna principles into practical use on an experimental basis. All concepts were tested thoroughly in order to make Huna a workable system that anyone could use. Reports of all experiments, research projects, and comparative studies were sent to members in the form of mimeographed bulletins, the *HRA Bulletins* (1948-1957) and the *Huna Vistas* (1958-1970). The current series, *Huna Vistas Newsletter*, was begun by Dr. Long shortly before his death in 1971. The second issue was a Memorial Issue and the third introduced the new director of the Huna work, Dr. E. Otha Wingo, whom Dr. Long had chosen three years before.

Members of HRA receive the *Huna Vistas Newsletter*, which is mailed four times a year. It contains news of current activities, lectures, conventions, new publications, group work, reviews of books, excerpts from letters, projects for research, and articles based on Huna and related concepts. Some issues are devoted to a survey of a single area.

Members are encouraged to participate in research projects and to share ideas and experiences, which may be reported in the *Huna Vistas Newsletter*. Articles for publication are also welcomed on a voluntary basis. The Huna Seminars provide opportunities to learn more about Huna and to meet Huna teachers and students.

The application forms for membership should be mailed to: Huna Research Associates, 126 Camellia Drive, Cape Girardeau, MO 63701.

Books by Max Freedom Long

Growing into Light. Marina del Rey: De Vorss, 1955. Simplified instructions to help the individual use Huna in daily life.

How Everything Was Made: Huna Stories for Children. Cape Girardeau: Huna Research, 1977. Mimeographed book of children's stories based on Huna.

HRA Bulletins and *Huna Vistas.* Cape Girardeau: Huna Research, n/d. The complete record of searches and researches by Max Freedom Long and the Huna Research Associates from 1948 to 1970. Included are 124 issues of HRA bulletins, 98 issues of Huna Vistas and 5 interim newsletters. Indexed.

Huna Code in Religions, The. Marina del Rey: De Vorss, 1965. The application of the Huna code to the unraveling of the secret teachings in the Gospels, Yoga and Buddhism with an abridged Hawaiian dictionary.

Introduction to Huna. Cottonwood, AZ: Esoteric Publications, 1975. The first publication on Huna in the United States. A good place to start the study of Huna. Preface and epilogue by Dr. E. Otha Wingo.

Mana, or Vital Force. Edited by Dr. E. Otha Wingo. 5th rev. edition. Cape Girardeau: Huna Research, 1976. Basic instructions in the accumulation and use of the vital force called *mana.*

Psychometric Analysis. Marina del Rey: De Vorss, 1959. The practical use of the pendulum for analysis based on Huna concepts. Codesheet for psychometric analysis readings included.

Recovering the Ancient Magic. Cape Girardeau: Huna Research, 1978. Exact reprint of the original Huna book.

Secret Science at Work, The. Marina del Rey: De Vorss, 1953. The practical application of the principles of Huna.

Secret Science behind Miracles. The. Marina del Rey: De Vorss, 1954. Complete story of the author's search and the uncovering of the lost keys to the ancient Huna System. Index.

Self-Suggestion. Marina del Rey: De Vorss, 1958. Teaches the reader to use self-suggestion according to the Huna System.

Short Talks on Huna. Cape Girardeau: Huna Research, 1978. Transcriptions of nine taped discussions on basic Huna concepts by Max Freedom Long.

Tarot Card Symbology. Edited by Dr. E. Otha Wingo. Cape Girardeau: Huna Research, 1972. A collection of articles from early issues of the *Huna Vistas.*

Other Huna Publications

Andrews, Lorrin. *A Dictionary of the Hawaiian Language.* Rutland, Vt.: Charles E. Tuttle, 1974. This reprint is the dictionary used by Max Freedom Long to decipher the coded Huna meanings of ancient Hawaiian roots. New introduction with author's original preface. An article on Polynesian languages by the eminent scholar, W. D. Alexander is included.

Glover, William R. *Huna: The Ancient Religion of Positive Thinking.* Cape Girardeau: Huna Research, 1979. Clear, concise account of the Huna philosophy, based on the taped lectures of Max Freedom Long and the author's experience in using them in classes.

Hoffman, Enid. *Huna: A Beginner's Guide.* Rockport, MA: Para Research, 1976. Practical, personal account of the author's experiences with Huna and other methods.

"Huna Centering and Energizing Techniques." Cape Girardeau: Huna Research, n/d. Cassette tape and booklet describing the technique and providing a guided form of meditation. 11 and 25 minutes.

Huna Vistas Newsletters. Cape Girardeau: Huna Research, n/d. Back issues of the current series from 1973. Special issues on biomagnetics, orgone energy, Huna harder, eliminating blocks and using Huna for healing.

Larson, Martin A. *The Essene-Christian Faith: A Study in the Sources of Western Religion.* New York: Philosophical Library, 1980. Scholarly, documented essential reading. The essence of over 1500 volumes on the Essenes and Dead Sea Scrolls. Complete revision and update of *The Essene Heritage.*

Larson, Martin A. *The Story of Christian Origins: The Source and Establishment of Western Religion.* Washington, D.C.: Joseph J. Binns/New Republic, 1977. Dr. Larson's masterpiece of research and comparison of the sources of all religions. Includes new, hardback edition of *The Religion of the Occident.*

Long, Max Freedom. *"How to Become a Magician." Cape Girardeau: Huna Research, 1975.*

Long, Max Freedom. *"The Need for Understanding of Huna and for the Use of Huna." lecture, 1957. Cape Girardeau: Huna Research, 1975.*

Melville, Leinani. *Children of the Rainbow: The Religion, Legends and Gods of pre-Christian Hawaii.* Wheaton, Ill.: Quest Books — Theosophical Publishing House, 1969. Discusses the esoteric code in the roots of the Hawaiian language. Includes illustrations of tapa cloth designs.

Rodman, Julius Scammon. *The Kahuna Sorcerers of Hawaii: Past and Present*. Smithtown, NY: Exposition Press, 1979. The result of forty-two years of research on kahuna lore. Includes a glossary of ancient religious terms and the books of the royal Hawaiian dead. The glossary is the collection of the late Leinani Melville Jones. Important for the study of the coded language of the kahuna.

Tregear, Edward. *The Maori-Polynesian Comparative Dictionary*. Oosterhout: Anthropological Publications, 1969. The most important research tool for the Huna code because it gives the history of root meanings in all the various Polynesian dialects.

Wingo, E. Otha. "Huna Psychology: An Introduction." Cape Girardeau: Huna Research, 1973. A 12 page summary of basic Huna concepts. Good to have when asked "What is Huna, anyway?"

Wingo, E. Otha. *Letters on Huna, The Fundamentals of Huna Psychology*. Cape Girardeau: Huna Research, 1980. Basic instructions for the practical use of Huna, the workable psychological system of the ancient Polynesians. This course of twelve lessons emphasizes the practical use of Huna in everyday life, basing the principles upon the researches and experiments of the thousands of Huna Research Associates under the direction of Dr. Long for nearly thirty years. All that you need to know to make the Huna system work for you is contained in this course.

Wingo, E. Otha. *Manual for Huna Groups*. Cape Girardeau: Huna Research, n/d. Suggestions for starting a Huna group and what to do at meetings. Revised as needed.

Wingo, E. Otha. "The Story of Huna Work." Cape Girardeau: Huna Research, n/d. A 16-page review of 100 years of Huna research.